PUBLISHED *by* PARABLES

Earthly Stories with a Heavenly Meaning

Jean,
Spread Your
Wings and Fly ♥

Anna Kay Schmidt

No matter what happens
in our life we know
we are more than
conquerors" Through
Him.
Romans 8:28

OUR SCARS OF HOPE

BY

ANNA KAY SCHMIDT

PUBLISHED by PARABLES
Earthly Stories with a Heavenly Meaning

Our Scars Of Hope
Anna Kay Schmidt

Published By Parables
February, 2019

ISBN 978-1-945698-93-4
Printed in the United States of America

Readers should be aware that Internet Web sites offered as citations and/or sources for further information may have been changed or disappeared between the time this was written and the time it is read.

Our Scars Of Hope

By

Anna Kay Schmidt

PUBLISHED by PARABLES
Earthly Stories with a Heavenly Meaning

This book is dedicated to
Gary J. Moore
who believed in me when I didn't
and saw something in me that I didn't know existed.
He was my friend, counselor, mentor and encourager.
He told me in December 1999 to keep a journal because, maybe
one day I might share my story with others.
Gary had been in a bus accident and suffered much with
his paralysis. He showed me and many others how to endure pain
with grace. He and his wife, Rhonda were a godsend to my
children and I during some of our darkest days. He also married
my husband, Larry and I.
I'll always remember him most graciously.
He's earned his reward and is now
pain-free and running with Jesus!
Thanks for the memories!
Love and miss you my friend!

TABLE OF CONTENTS

Our Scars Of Hope

INTRODUCTION

Scars. Some small, some big. A reminder of an accident, a surgery, a fight, a fall, or a sports injury. For one reason or another, we all have scars and may notice them every day. But, what about the scars inside, deep inside that have hurt us to the core of our being? Those times that have left us speechless, breathless, sleepless, tearless, motionless and mostly, hopeless. No one sees the hidden scars that we've battled. Maybe if we had a physical wound or a scar, someone might ask what happened, might console, might understand, or possibly care. But, they can't see it, so they don't, and we hurt and suffer alone.

Have you been in this place? Maybe you're here now... searching for an answer or a reason to go on and deal with the hurt and pain. You may think as I did, no one understands or 'gets it', and you feel alone.

The stories in this book are from myself and other ladies that have been hurt and wounded in life. We want others to know that there are people that understand the hidden wounds because we've lived them. The desire from each of us, is that you will find comfort and hope from the different wound stories that we've experienced along our life journey in this book.

These stories are real. It's not easy opening up our wounds, and past hurts, and sharing them on these pages, but we believe that the short remembrance of the pain we experienced in writing our story, could benefit and help someone who's hurting right now. Could it be for you? As Esther said in the Bible, "Who knows whether you have not come to the kingdom for such a time as this?" Esther 4:14b (ESV)

Chapter 1

MY STORY – MY SONG

Rhonda Love Moore

With reservation, the man entered our room and paused before asking, "Are you ready?" In the silence that followed, the ventilator suddenly became the focus. "Take all the time you need," he responded, "I'll return when you're ready." Would I ever be ready to disconnect the machine keeping my husband alive? After forty-one-years of marriage I faced the final few minutes with him on this earth. My only solace was his freedom from earthly suffering and my faith in God's promise that he would soon be with God, his Creator. Grief hung over the room like a dark cloud.

"I waited patiently for the Lord to help me, and he turned to me and heard my cry. He lifted me out of the pit of despair, out of the mud and the mire. He set my feet on solid ground and steadied me as I walked along. He has given me a new song to sing, a hymn of praise to our God. Many will see what he has done and be amazed. They will put their trust in the Lord." Psalm 40:1-3 NLT

Too soon an RN returned, and I knew it was time to let him go. For several hours, our family; my three children, their mates and grandchildren had comforted him with hope-filled scriptures, joyful songs of praise and many memories filled with laughter and tears. Surrounded by family who cherished him completely, he took his final breath as we knew he was ushered into the presence of his Father Creator, whose Word had assured us of such hope.

We waited for them to reverently carry his body away before we allowed ourselves to breathe normally. Reality brought me back to the cluttered hospital room. The scattered supplies and overflowing trash containers were stark reminders of all the devastating pain and suffering that had consumed our lives for twenty-six years. I wondered how I would survive the clutter and darkness inside me threatening to drown me in despair and grief. My only hope was in God, who had sustained me countless times in my life.

"When you go through deep waters, I will be with you. When you go through rivers of difficulty, you will not drown. When you walk through the fires of oppression, you will not be burned up; the flames will not consume you."
Isaiah 43:2 ESV

On another day twenty-six years ago, when this began, I also needed God and his promises to sustain me and my family.

January 5, 1987 - My husband woke early as usual to begin his day with a five-mile jog in our quiet farming community in Oklahoma. After a shower and a kiss for me and our children, he was off to drive his school bus route of sixteen students. Becoming an orphan at age ten had helped him have compassion for kids and everyone in need. After his morning route, he would eagerly begin his other passion; serving as a minister of our church. His love for the people equaled his devotion to me, our two daughters, ages thirteen and eleven, and our son age nine. Every day for the past fifteen years he had served the Lord in other ministries with the same joy he had that morning.

At 8:00 AM that crisp January morning he picked up his sixteenth passenger three miles outside of town and was headed back when a speeding pickup and his school bus collided. The bus rolled several times landing in a wheat field where his body lay lifeless after being ejected through the windshield. His spinal cord was severed, leaving him paralyzed from the waist down. He was thirty-five years old.

After a brief diagnosis at the local hospital, I watched the flight-for-life helicopter lift-up, taking him to the nearest trauma center hundreds of miles away. I had to force my despondent spirit up as well...to the only One who could provide the hope and help we needed.

10

"I look up to the mountains-does my help come from there? My help comes from the Lord, who made heaven and earth! The Lord himself watches over you! The Lord stands beside you as your protective shade." Psalm 121:1-2, 5 NLT

That day and in the weeks to come I couldn't foresee the extent of the life-altering changes we faced, but from the first moment I heard the deafening ambulance sirens in our quiet farming community, I did know this truth: whoever needs help right now; God knows, and He is able to be the refuge for their every need. In the months that followed I knew in my head that God was my refuge, but soon waves of trials and stress began to burn up my physical and spiritual strength. I needed to be with both my husband and children who were three hundred and sixty-five miles apart for seven months. I found it almost impossible to lift my weary, broken heart to God in prayer. Like a child alone in the dark I often failed to see that my Father God was just one cry away waiting with all the comfort and help I needed. God will allow the darkness to reveal His Light.

The accident left my husband's body shattered and his spirit crushed. While in rehab and when he returned home, the constant nerve pain and trauma left him doubting his ability to provide for his family, to continue his church ministry, and even his desire to live at times. His deep faith and positive attitude had sustained him all his life, but the injuries and daily struggles left him broken. He had been my rock, my decision maker and spiritual guide, and now unequipped and fearful, we began to unravel. But God was faithful to meet our needs. He was at work through many people who helped lift us up.

"God is our refuge and strength, a very present help in trouble...though the mountains be moved into the heart of the sea and the waters roar...we will not fear...for He is with us." Psalms 46:1, 3; 23:4 ESV

Our loving church and entire community supported us in many ways. The church continued paying our salary during the four months of rehab in Denver, Colorado and again during rehab in Texas for three months. They assured my husband that his job as the minister was waiting for him "when" he returned, "even" from his wheelchair. Their support and love continued every day of the following seven years he ministered there from his wheelchair despite the chronic pain, depression, multiple surgeries, illnesses and mind-altering side-effects of multiple medications. Several families "adopted" our children the many times they couldn't be with me as I traveled to rehab hospitals in Oklahoma, Colorado and Texas.

This was a trying time for our children who were resilient, but also affected deeply by the battle scars of trauma. We continually prayed for our children, whose lives today reveal God's faithful care over them. Their faith in God, perseverance in adversity and amazing compassion for those in need are evidences of God's everlasting love for all his children. God is so faithful! The seven months spent in rehab and the years of adjustment back home were dark and fearful in many ways, but at the same time they were filled with treasures of God's presence and his amazing love. I'm convinced that the darkness served to reveal the Light of God's love that planted seeds of faith and hope in me, our family, and many others still today who hear of God's abundant faithfulness through our story.

While in rehab our small, church family built us a new, beautifully handicapped-accessible home with the help of more volunteers from the community who donated labor and materials. Upon completion, they gave us the keys and said, "This is yours for as long as you desire." We tearfully and thankfully received their gift of love and God's provision. God was so faithful!

We did our best to adjust to the new "normal" when the months of rehab were completed. My husband was independent in his physical care but his inability to manage the pain and function at the level he desired began to drain the life from within him. The stress of seeing him suffer physically and emotionally, and concerns for our future with three young dependents began to threaten my well-being. I watched him attempt the impossible from early morning to late at night to maintain his ministry and meet the needs of our family. His sheer determination and faith in God gave him strength to keep going. Friends and faithful workers in our church, along with our gifted Dr. were blessings. God's mercies were endless, and we were thankful.

"But this I call to mind, and therefore I have hope: The steadfast love of the Lord never ceases; his mercies never come to an end; they are new every morning; great is your faithfulness. The Lord is my portion, says my soul, therefore I will hope in him." Lamentations 3:18-24 ESV

My hope was in God's ability to provide, but exhaustion and depression began to overwhelm me. As our children moved into their teen years, active in sports, school activities and time with friends, I struggled to balance family needs, a part-time job and church activities at the same time. Often, I felt like my family and friends were all on a speeding train toward destinations while I was still back at the station holding onto the ticket counter wanting everything to slow down and allow me to catch up.

But life moved on whether I was on the train or not. Stress and fatigue affected my memory and ability to function properly. Anti-depressants prescribed by our family Dr. were ineffective, so I believed the myth that it was my fault; it was a faith issue, not a medication issue. This myth and my fears from what I saw the medications doing to my husband's ability to function left me vulnerable and despondent. Only God's loving arms wrapped around me and my family continuously enabled us to survive this dark and fearful journey.

In 1993, after twelve years in our small farming community environment, we faced something we couldn't ignore. My husband's deteriorating health left him struggling to keep up with full-time ministry demands, family needs, and hours of his own physical care related to spinal cord injury. His deep faith and positive attitude enabled him to look past these "setbacks", as he saw them, to see a future God would make clear. Motivational speaking, writing, and family counseling was the path he saw God opening to him. Relocating near Denver, Colorado, where his medical specialists were located, as well as ministry opportunities seemed the logical choice. God provided a positive outlook despite fears of the unknown and our personal family obstacles. God's faithfulness in our lives drove us forward. Our church leaders had gifted us with our amazing house, and now it was ours to sell as we began anew in Colorado. What a blessing God provides through faithful servants.

"Trust in the Lord with all your heart; do not depend on your own understanding. Seek his will in all you do, and he will show you the right path to take." Proverbs 3:5, 6 NLT

In our new Colorado home, far from the support we'd grown to depend on, many overwhelming challenges arose. Life continued for our two teens still at home with us. Challenges and new opportunities opened for them in a school whose enrollment equaled the entire population of our community in Oklahoma. Our middle daughter found the amazing path God had set for her despite huge obstacles. She soon met her future husband at church and today after twenty-one-years of marriage and three amazing children, I continue to thank God for His loving care over them. Our son also saw his challenges as opportunities to grow as he excelled in everything he took on in high school and then in college. Today he shares life with his beautiful wife and amazing twins. My heart ached daily for our eldest daughter who chose to put college on hold for a year and remain in Oklahoma near our soon-to-be son-in-law. But I could put my fears at rest as I saw God's loving Hand upon her and our son-in-law. They soon married and moved near us in Colorado, where today, after twenty-four years of marriage and two lovely granddaughters, we still see God at work in their lives.

We were thankful for our new church family in Colorado despite their lack of insight and ability to meet the emotional and spiritual needs within our family. As painful as this was for our family, it gave our family eyes of compassion and tender hearts for those with special needs we may never have acquired without the pain.

My husband worked as a counselor, motivational speaker and writer. He pushed himself for weeks at a time and then would crash with exhaustion and pain. Despite my fears and advice to slow down, he began to travel excessively throughout the country speaking at seminars, churches and businesses. My concerns led to fears for his health and the needs of our active teens at home. This and my own fatigue and job demands took me back into a dark place. Being in an unfamiliar large city and church where I failed to connect with personal and spiritual support, I began to isolate and become unable to cope with daily life. I mistakenly allowed frustration to grow toward my husband, the counselor who I expected to heal the brokenness in our lives and inside me. I was so broken! I failed to call on my God; the true Counselor who alone can heal my broken spirit.

"The Lord hears his people when they call to him for help...The Lord is close to the brokenhearted; he rescues those whose spirits are crushed." Psalm 34:17:18 NLT

God makes a way when we cannot find our way; when we open ourselves to his help and mercy. Our teen daughter's youth group was having a weekend retreat in the nearby Rocky Mountains. I volunteered to be a sponsor. On a quiet walk with another mom I had learned to trust, I shared some of my problems. She shared the name of a local Christian Counselor and suggested I call for an appointment and I reluctantly agreed. By Monday when she suspected I would back out, she called and said she'd made me an appointment for the following day, what a blessing! I was thankful that God had opened the way to the beginning of true healing for years of brokenness in my life.

"This is my comfort in my affliction, that your promise, (O, God) gives me life. You are my hiding place and my shield; I hope in your word." Psalm 119:50, 114 ESV

The counselor helped me through grief I had carried from childhood through the time of my husband's accident. Through God, she began to unravel years of abuse. She led me to a grace-filled Bible study group where for the first time in my life I had a relationship with my God of grace. He opened my heart and filled me with joy, hope, forgiveness, grace and love I had never known before.

As speaking demands grew for my husband and his failing physical health mounted, his ability to manage and cope failed. My doubts concerning the new psychiatrist he was seeing should have prompted me to action, but I failed to act in time. Depression intensified, and the medication's adverse effect brought on the suicidal thoughts he couldn't overcome. I came home one day and found him unconscious next to an empty bottle of pills and a suicide note. Months in the mental hospital, numerous new medications and multiple shock treatments left him as someone I would never fully know as my husband again. I tried to process the pain of his lifeless self. Would he ever return? Would life ever be "normal" again? Where was God in all this twilight zone? One night as I pulled into my driveway after the forty-mile drive home from the hospital, I couldn't remember driving at all! Fear and grief clouded out all reasoning. I cried out to God on my knees begging to know He was with us, pleading for His Presence of peace in my life.

Returning home from the mental hospital, my husband was suffering more than I could bear. With God's help, we slowly returned to a daily routine and saw gradual healing of his mind, but his ability to be independent was failing. His strong will for independence brought on a struggle to keep him safe from bad choices. During times of overwhelming stress, the verbal and emotional abuse I inflicted on my husband was unbelievable. His pain was increasing, and medications robbed him of the ability to function. The medical field was unable to help, and our willing children had no answers either. In desperation, I begged God to be merciful and take him and us both to our eternal home free from pain and suffering and to free our children from further suffering as well. This unhealthy thinking created guilt that drove me into spiritual darkness where little hope remained. I tried anti-depressants again to no avail. I isolated completely except for my family and attended worship only on occasion. Depression, anger and spiritual darkness consumed me. Love for my husband, my children and grandchildren, as well as my deep convictions kept me from taking my own life. I turned to foolish choices for comfort. For years, I intoxicated myself with alcohol to dull the pain. I knew I had reached the bottom. But as always, God made a way out. His love never fails.

One day our mail contained a newsletter from a pastor in California who shared his story of grief, pain and bad choices. His words of comfort and help convicted me of my addiction and lack of trust in my Father God who loved me and was waiting for me to turn to him for help and comfort.

"In my distress, I called to the LORD; I prayed to my God for help. He heard me from his sanctuary; my cry to him reached his ears." Psalm 18:6 NLT

God led me to a recovery support group for every hurt, habit, and hang-up. I completed the twelve-step program and was working on healing and recovery. As I experienced the joy of recovery and God's presence, I knew I could handle any trial with God and support from others who shared life's pain and recovery. Soon the testing of my trust in God became a reality.

One afternoon, as I was away for a brief time, my husband fell while attempting a transfer into his handicapped van. Unable to move with a broken femur, hip and other injuries, he laid for hours on the garage floor until he could crawl to his phone. His multiple injuries required inpatient care at a long-term facility, but his insurance covered only a brief stay. His pain and fear brought on hostility toward me and anyone who attempted to manage his care. We faced a financial crisis and a future with more questions than answers. God provided our three adult children to come to our aid in such a loving way, I will eternally be grateful to God for them and their spouses. The decision was made to move my husband and myself to the Oklahoma City area where our son and his wife would help care for us. I was joyful and thankful to be near our son and daughter-in-law and soon-to-be-born-twins, but filled with anxiety of the unknown and with grief for leaving my daughters and grandchildren behind in Colorado; the comfort I'd learned to depend on. God was calling me to a new chapter in my life, a new testing of my faith in him as I'd never been tested before.

Eight short months after we arrived in Oklahoma, we found ourselves in ICU fighting for my husband's life. His tired, fragile body couldn't fight the complications of an ileostomy and other multiple issues his body had fought for twenty-six years. The ICU surgeons regretfully, but bluntly informed us that my husband wouldn't survive the needed surgery and without a ventilator, he wouldn't live but a short time. They asked him who would decide when the ventilator would be removed, and he looked to me and nodded his answer. The doctors and nurses confirmed his answer; I was to make the decision. Surrounded by family, in the presence of our loving God, we could shower him with love and comfort the last three days of his life.

My husband never doubted God's love for him or his Sovereign Will over the events in his life. He followed the passion in his heart to share the good news of God's love for all people. He loved everyone he met and everyone who met him adored him. He left a legacy for his children and grandchildren to follow that we can all be thankful and proud of. I miss him every day after four years without him, but I praise God along with my children that he is safe in the arms of God with his Savior Jesus Christ.

My journey continues. God continually provides ways for healing and connection with good people. I have loving support from my children, my family, my church, support groups, counseling and precious dear friends. I have a long way to go, but I'm healing, and on the way to finding God's plan for my life. The trials of my life left scars and wounds that only God can heal if I allow him to transform me from the woman who saw herself as a victim in darkest hopelessness, into a woman of Faith who knows I am powerless, but not helpless. At times I'm desperately lonely, but never alone. In the darkest times, my constant Light is God's Word, his comfort through his creation, and his good people in everyday situations. His love is everlasting, love never fails.

I recall the words of a friend years ago during a very dark time in my life. "Dear friend," he said, "God has put a song in your heart. In his time, he will reveal the words, the notes and enable you to sing it. God will enable you to sing his purpose for your life."

When I was a small girl, I dreamed of being an opera singer. I would practice in front of the mirror and joyfully perform as if before a live audience. Life can distort and sabotage our dreams but can never take away our hope of fulfilling them. Only we can do that.

"Sing to the Lord a new song; sing to the Lord, all the earth."
Psalm 96:1 ESV

Today, one of my greatest joys is to listen to and watch my children and grandchildren sing. They sing praises to God in church and home, they sing as they work, and they sing silly songs as they dance and make me laugh. I'm learning to sing again. I may never sing in the opera, but every day I am blessed to be alive, I am singing with all my heart to the One who put a song, a purpose, eternal hope and joy in my heart the day he formed me in my mother's womb.

"For the Lord your God is living among you. He is a mighty savior. He will take delight in you with gladness. With his love, he will calm all your fears. He will rejoice over you with joyful songs." Zephaniah 3:17

To God be the glory over all the earth.

Chapter 2

A Chance to Live

I have a wedding wall in my house. There are pictures of my four children as smiling newlyweds, and more recently, my four grandchildren. Everyone looks happy and healthy, which is a great victory. Just looking at those pictures, no one would know that daily medications are keeping my daughter and granddaughter alive and well. Both were diagnosed with life-threatening illnesses when they were very young, and both of their childhoods are filled with memories of hospitals and injections.

My daughter was five years old when she was diagnosed with Type 1 Diabetes, or Juvenile Diabetes. My husband and I also had a two year old son and I was expecting our third child in two months. I noticed that she was more thirsty than usual, but I thought it was because the weather was getting warmer. One night I heard her get up about 12 times to use the bathroom, and I knew something was wrong. When I saw a rash on her stomach the next morning, I called the doctor and made an appointment to have it checked. I had no idea how our lives were going to change that day.

As the doctor was looking at the rash, I mentioned the other symptoms and he ordered a blood test. A normal blood glucose level is 80-120, and hers was over 600. He wanted us to go immediately to Vanderbilt Children's Hospital, but I needed to make arrangements for my son, and to pack our bags, so he let us go home first. Of course, I was in shock. I called my husband and all I could say was, "I need you." My sweet friend who thought she would be keeping my son for a couple of hours, took care of him until my parents arrived from Georgia and picked him up later that night.

My daughter was in the hospital for a week, while they gave her insulin and taught us how to give her injections. Even my father learned to give injections since he would be the back-up person when I was ready to have the baby. I told the nurses that if I went in labor, they could just wheel me downstairs! On the day we brought her home, I felt like I was bringing a new baby home. I was so afraid that I would do something wrong. She had a very strict diet and needed two injections a day, which was hard to explain to a five-year-old. A few weeks later, we did bring a new baby home. By the providence of God, my parents had bought the house across the street from us because they were thinking of moving to be near their grandchildren. They were able to help me with the children during the day and go to their house at night. Between my daughter's eating and injection schedule, an active two-year-old and a new baby, we were exhausted!

There were many challenges to overcome after my daughter's diagnosis. We had to learn how to celebrate holidays without sugar. In 1988, there were not many sugar-free options available, so for Halloween we bought her a bag of candy just for her. When there were parties at school, I always sent sugar-free Jell-O squares and sometimes that was the only thing she could eat. On her sixth birthday, I frosted an angel food cake with Cool Whip, and I was concerned that the other children would not like it, but they loved it. One girl even asked her mother to get the recipe! Those little victories were so encouraging.

One of the biggest challenges we faced was the beginning of the school year. I was prepared each year to "educate" the teacher about diabetes. When my daughter was going into fifth grade, we moved to another town and I was very nervous about the new school. I went to meet the teacher and had my information ready to share when I noticed that she was wearing a medic alert necklace. She also had diabetes, and I knew that God had worked that out for us.

During those stressful days, when I tried to imagine what my daughter's future would be like, I could only see darkness. How would having diabetes affect the rest of her life? Would she ever get married and have children? Would people treat her differently? I tried hard to keep her life as normal as possible. I didn't want her to see herself as "sick" even though she had a chronic illness. What I did not know is that God was preparing her to face a battle for her own child's life many years later. He also took care of my fears for her future. She married a wonderful man, became a nurse, lived in Peru as a missionary, and had two beautiful children. This is where my granddaughter's story begins.

My daughter's pregnancies were considered high risk because of her diabetes. They were living in Peru at the time, so they made the decision to return to the States for the birth of their first child. They had a beautiful little girl with no complications. When my daughter became pregnant with their son, they returned to the States for the birth but this time things did not go as planned. My grandson was born five weeks early and spent two weeks in the NICU. Just a few weeks before he was born, my granddaughter had her two year check-up, and everything looked fine, but because she had a slight heart murmur when she was born, her doctor wanted her to have a heart echo before they returned to Peru. They had only been home a week with the new baby when the echo was scheduled at Vanderbilt Children's Hospital.

I was working as a church secretary at that time and at 4:00 when I was getting ready to go home, the phone rang. It was my son-in-law and I remember him saying, "There's no easy way to say this, so I'm just going to say it." He told me that my granddaughter's heart was fine, but they were on the cancer floor. The technician went a little too low during the test and saw a mass in her abdomen. She was diagnosed with stage three Hepatoblastoma, which is liver cancer. She received two rounds of chemo at Vanderbilt, but the oncologist knew after her first scan that it was not working. She was put on the transplant list and transferred to Pittsburgh Children's Hospital, where she continued having chemo to stop the cancer from spreading.

It was so hard to know how to pray during this time of waiting. We wanted our sweet girl to live, but we knew that someone else's child would have to die for that to happen. We could only pray for God's will to be done. The prayers of our family, friends and hundreds of people we did not even know surrounded us and encouraged us. Almost two months after she was put on the transplant list, the call came that a liver was available. We will always be thankful for that family who lost their child and made the choice to save another child through organ donation.

After her surgery, my granddaughter spent two months in the hospital recovering from the transplant. During the first week she had four major surgeries due to complications with the bile ducts. Each time she had surgery, even the doctors did not know what the outcome would be or if the transplant would be successful. She also had two more rounds of chemo to make sure all the cancer cells were gone. She continued to have complications with the bile ducts for the next two years and made many trips back to Pittsburgh for procedures. She has had several rejection episodes, which require the use of steroids, and she will always have to take immunosuppressant drugs. The chemo caused hearing loss and terrible side effects, which was hard to explain to a two-year-old. The good news is that now her liver function is almost normal, and she is a survivor.

According to Philippians 4:4-7, joy should be part of a Christian's daily life, but there were many days when we did not feel like rejoicing. Watching my daughter learn to live with diabetes and my granddaughter suffer with the side effects of chemo was painful. How is it possible to rejoice when we are going through trials? When I look back on the lives of my daughter and granddaughter, one thing is certain: God was always with us.

I believe that when we go through trials, we need to share what we learned with others, and, most of all, we need to give God the glory for what He has done for us. The first lesson I learned is that, without a doubt, nothing is impossible with God. Matthew 19:26 says "With men this is impossible, but with God all things are possible." My granddaughter is living proof of this!

Secondly, "the peace of God, which surpasses all understanding" in Philippians 4:7 is real. When my daughter and her husband were listening to the doctors' talk about the uncertainty of the surgeries they were performing, they felt that peace. They knew that God was in control, and they trusted Him.

Third, God's timing really is perfect. It amazes me to look back and see how God was working in our lives. The heart echo that went too low and found my granddaughter's tumor was not an accident! He provided what we needed at the time we needed it most. Philippians 4:19 says "And my God shall supply all your need according to His riches in glory by Christ Jesus."

Fourth, other people are watching and it is an opportunity to show others our faith. We had such a large amount of mail that our mailman began bringing it to the door and he always asked about our granddaughter. In fact, his mother made a quilt for her. Many people have told us what an inspiration our granddaughter is to them, and how they continue to pray for her. I Peter 1:7 tells us "that the genuineness of your faith, being much more precious than gold that perishes, though it is tested by fire, may be found to praise, honor, and glory at the revelation of Jesus Christ."

And last, even when life is uncertain, we can rejoice in the Lord always. He has promised in Romans 8:28 that "all things work together for good to those who love God, to those who are called according to His purpose." This does not mean that the outcome is always what we want. Children die from cancer every day. Why was our granddaughter's life saved when others are not? Only God knows the answer to that question.

We know that Genesis 1:31 tells us "God saw everything He had made, and it was very good." We know that when Adam and Eve sinned, that brought sickness, disease and death into the world. We know this, but when bad things happen to people we love, it is still hard to understand. Trusting in God's promises will build our faith and make us stronger when our faith is tested. Our family found comfort and hope in Ephesians 3:20-21, "Now to Him who is able to do exceedingly abundantly above all that we ask or think, according to the power that works in us, to Him be glory in the church by Christ Jesus to all generations, forever and ever. Amen."

Chapter 3

His Plan, Not Mine

I'm 55 years old now. By all appearances, I look to be a normal, healthy wife and mother. I'm pleased when someone will remark that I look "normal". Even though I may look this way, I am anything but. I have spent most of my adult life fighting an incurable rare disease. Despite two different types of surgery and countless medications, I am considered "non-responsive to treatment".

As a child, I was normal. I experienced the usual child -hood illnesses. My father, a physician, always made sure that my sisters, and I stayed up to date with immunizations and regular blood work.

When I was 18, I began working for a national retail store as a cashier during the Christmas season. I didn't realize right away but one of the stock boys had noticed me and wanted to ask me for a date. After a time, Bryan and I began dating and eventually married two years later. I had just completed my Associates Degree, but because my lifelong dream had always been to be a wife and mother, I couldn't see myself studying further to receive my Bachelors. In my mind, it wasn't necessary because I had accomplished my dream of marrying. Eventually, we would begin having children, if that was God's plan for us. It was our dream.

Ahhhhh, "God's plan". If there's one thing I've learned in life, it's that His plan is so often not our plan. In fact, I would have to say that rarely does it go as you think it will. That can be an awesome and beautiful thing if we allow Him to have His way with us. He is, after all, the Master of all things. Most times, us regular folk think we have life all under control. That was me. I'd married one of the nicest, most handsome Christian guys there ever was. We had a great marriage and eventually Bryan was able to finish college after time spent in the military. We both worked as we lived in the small town where I was raised. They weren't "great" jobs, and we struggled to make ends meet, but my God, My Shepherd King, always made sure our needs were met.

Even as a child, I had suffered from headaches from time to time. In 1991, they began to worsen. I mentioned it to my dad, who had been practicing medicine since 1962, in this same small town. Thinking I might have some sinus blockage, he thought an X-ray was in order. I did have slight blockage, but what also showed up in addition to that, floored him. A very large tumor centered in the middle of my brain. As a physician, he had seen many tumors. As a Daddy, never! To this day, I can't imagine how this affected him. He cleared his patient schedule and began accompanying me to numerous appointments.

The news of my tumor was hard on Bryan, my sisters, my dad and my mama. My parents divorced when I was 16 and my mom hadn't remarried. She worked hard to support herself and couldn't afford to take very many days off of work. Because she loved me so much and had always been a devoted mother to me and my sisters, I knew she would take as much time off as possible. My sisters lived a few hours away, but supported me long distance. I felt much loved, but I worried about the toll this had to be taking on my family.

After a series of appointments with many types of doctors, surgery to remove the tumor was finally scheduled. I was admitted the night before and family from both sides arrived to support us through this difficult time. The next day, as I was wheeled out of my room, dozens of people from our church lined the hallway to show support for what would turn into a 10-hour surgery.

After I awakened, in the Surgical Intensive Care Unit, I saw my family surrounding me. Visiting hours were limited, so I was alone most of that time. I mostly slept, but I remember seeing my mama check on me at 3:20 AM. She and Bryan spent the night in the ICU waiting room as neither wanted to be far away. Not long after I watched her disappear and the door to my room close, I fell asleep. Soon, I was awakened by the worst head pain I have ever experienced. I cried out for a nurse and she appeared immediately, calling me by name. I sat up and that's the last I remember until waking up to doctors and nurses lining both sides of my bed. I knew that whatever had happened to me, had taken place in the middle of the night. Because of that, seeing my surgeon standing there alarmed me. I knew something serious had taken place, and he had been called at home, but I wasn't sure what. They explained that I had stopped breathing, but because I was so near the nurse's station they were able to hear my cries of help, which allowed them to reach me quickly. A "Code Blue" alert had been sent out over the PA system and I had survived. Little did I know then, but my life would never be the same.

What had happened to me was a mystery to everyone. Tests were run to determine the cause but nothing definite showed. Within 48 hours of my ordeal, I began feeling very sick and my entire body ached. I had developed Chemical Meningitis, which earned me a month-long stay in the hospital. I was very weak and slept most of the time.

After being released from my long stay in the hospital, I recovered a bit longer at home before returning to work. I felt fine, and it was good to be back in my daily routine. Even though I felt well, at times I would get severe head pain that would last approximately 30 seconds. I was confused but never told anyone. I had a routine MRI to confirm if all of my tumor had been removed during surgery. Bryan took off work, and we went to my appointment. After my scan was over and I was allowed to leave. I was later notified that the MRI revealed a "giant aneurysm" that had already bled and I should return to the hospital ASAP. I was scared! Three months had passed since my tumor surgery and I was back in the hospital again.

I endured another 10-hour surgery. Bryan and my family were informed that I had survived the aneurysm repair but warned that I might not know who anyone is and could possibly have paralysis on my left side. Lots and lots of prayers were said on my behalf and God allowed me to not only live to tell my story but to do so without any of what had been predicted by doctors.

My recovery was much less with this surgery and I again returned to work. I can't say that I felt very well because I had a headache that never seemed to go away. They lingered on for so long that I had to quit working. Bryan made the decision for us to move away from our small town so that I wouldn't have to work, and he could make more money to live on. We found ourselves in a large city with plenty of doctors to choose from but none of them could determine why I felt the way I did. God's decision for me to suffer with illness, lasted 12 long years. Each and every day I suffered with a headache. I was able to function most days, but some days were spent in bed. We felt that our dream to have children would not be obtained. With the way I felt each day, I wouldn't have been able to care for them properly. Several times, I thanked Him for sparing me from experiencing the aggravation of having children that needed the tender love and care that I couldn't give them. God doesn't make mistakes and His decision for us to be childless, was no exception.

As my 30s came and went, I was no closer to having a normal life. How I longed to be 28 again. I had worked full time and walked 5 miles a day to stay in shape. I was physically strong and loved helping Bryan do things that required strength. There wasn't anything I couldn't do, and I felt great! I definitely took that life for granted.

During a routine visit to one of my doctors, she mentioned a new physician that I should consider seeing. I made the appointment and went for my first visit. Within minutes, she diagnosed me with a rare incurable disease but assured me that it was treatable. Soon after, I began the medication she prescribed and within seconds, my headache of 12 long years, disappeared. I couldn't help but cry with excitement and thankfulness. God had found this doctor for me and He had lifted the burden of experiencing incredible pain that would not go away.

Life was good again!!! I had essentially lost 12 years of my life and I had lots to make up for. I enrolled in water exercise and Bryan and I began living life on the active and fun side again. We could finally join groups at church and they could count on us to be there. Twelve years is a long time to wait upon the Lord. I can't claim that I was patient and trusting, because I wasn't. I tried to never feel sorry for myself, but at times, I did. I wanted to feel good again.

God hears our every prayer and knows our every desire. Everything is in His timing, ALWAYS. He knew that since the age of 12, my dream was to marry and have children. One morning I began feeling sick and dizzy. I was 41 and had experienced numerous health issues, so it only made sense to think that something else could be wrong. The idea of being pregnant never crossed my mind. However, my God, my Shepherd King blessed us with a beautiful baby girl that we named after my mama's mother. She was born healthy and didn't inherit any of my medical problems. She's a normal healthy teenager now. Bryan and I thank God each and every day for our Little Miracle. That night so long ago, when God spared my life, He knew what we didn't. That one day, we would be living the dream of being parents.

When I thought my life was taken, the Good Lord blessed us by giving us a child.

Chapter 4

My Cancer Blessing?

One month before I turned 45 years old, I found a lump in my left breast while doing my self-exam in the shower. Immediately I called my family doctor to schedule an appointment. He told me to come in right then, which I did. My doctor couldn't find it himself, so I directed him to my findings. That same day he scheduled a mammogram followed by another more defined mammogram. There were low whispers as people scurried up and down the hall. I knew not to jump ahead and draw my own conclusions, so I grabbed a magazine and began copying down pizza recipes six total, of which I still have never tried…complete and total distractions.

IT HAS LEGS

Now it was time for my ultrasound. As I lay there on the table I was overcome by anxiety. What will she find? I began to pray and calm myself, breathing deeply as I had been taught in my Lamaze classes. God gave me some hymns of praise to help me be at peace. Now the Diagnostic Medical Sonographer/Ultrasound Technician was all set to begin the ultrasound. The gel was cold as she placed the transducer probe on my breast. I lost all sense of modesty. Who cares? The room could have been full of people. I have to know and I have to know now! My positioning was such that I had a full view of the screen. There it was! I calmly and quietly exclaimed, "Oh, no! It has legs!" I knew then it was breast cancer. Tears began to run down my face and flood into my ears. The technician quickly turned the screen from my view. Really? Did she think I would 'un-see' it? She noticed my tears and my stifled crying. (Maybe it wasn't as stifled as I thought.) Down the hall she flew loudly proclaiming to her superior what had happened. I heard a low calm voice though I couldn't make out one word. A more 'weathered' technician entered and looked only at the monitor. She completed the ultrasound in its entirety. As she gently placed her hand on my forearm and looked into my eyes, she informed me that the doctor would have my results immediately and I should go back to his office and stay until he could go over the findings with me. She had kind and caring eyes. I know God sent her to me. She left the room. I got dressed. All the while I doubted my own eyes, well, maybe some tumors with 'legs' are benign.

The doctor's clinic was walking distance from the hospital. When I walked in and told the lady at the desk that I had been instructed to stay until I consulted with the doctor over my test findings, she told me my doctor was out for the remainder of the day. I stood there dumbfounded. All logic left me as I bombarded her with "What should I do now? They told me to come straight here and wait until I saw the doctor." Bless her heart. She had to tell me to go home and wait until the doctor called me TOMORROW with the results. Not once, but twice! I left the office still in a daze. Questions and thoughts kept racing through my head. Tomorrow? I can't wait until tomorrow! The world must stop. I must know now! What will I tell my family? Who should I call first?

As I pulled up into the driveway, I collected myself to go in and face my three Home-schooled children. They all three burst out the door and ran to the car to greet me. What pleasantry! We went into the house and I called my husband, Kevin to come home. Lunch is served. They all knew why I had gone to the Doctor. After lunch I asked them to come and sit on the couch, and I laid out my morning happenings. Needless to say, school was out for the day. Instead, we watched movies and played outside. It was a perfect fall day. Kevin went back to the office. I called Mom. She, in turn, called my five siblings. We all prayed and waited the night for 'The Call' the next morning. In retrospect, we ALL needed the night to ready ourselves for the inevitable news.

It was nearly noon the next day when I received a call from the nurse confirming my breast cancer diagnosis. They had already set up an appointment for me to meet with a surgeon to obtain a biopsy. I hung up the phone and called Kevin. It was hardest to call my Mom. She, herself, had a near death experience just five years earlier. Her health still wasn't the best. Would the news that her oldest girl had breast cancer stir up her health issues again? None the less, she was my next call. I conveyed a message the nurse had instructed me to give. All female relatives should immediately schedule a mammogram.

Our closest Cancer Center was less than 20 miles away. Requests for mammogram records had been sent from all my previous mammograms and breast examinations. The surgeon viewed my last mammogram and its report. Then he asked me, "So why when your report read 'Not yet clinically significant calcification processes' did you not get something done?" I reached into my folder and pulled out my last mammogram report received, which read "Normal Mammogram." His eyes widened in amazement and whispered "Oh!" At that point he stepped out into the hall to speak with his 'class'. (It was a teaching hospital.) I heard him say I had nothing that had appeared on the cancer warning signs list. I didn't drink. I never smoked. There was no sign of breast cancer in my family. Nothing on the list matched with my diagnosis. Absolutely nothing! The biopsy was taken. Surgery was scheduled the day before my 45th birthday…less than one month away.

IT'S JUST NOT FAIR

How could this happen to me? I am a Medical Technologist/Research Scientist! I was keenly aware of the value of medically preventative maintenance programs. I was the one who always recommended to be tested regularly and exactly, when I should…annual checkups, bloodwork, and chest x-rays. My baseline mammogram was at age 35. I had annual mammograms. I never missed! NEVER! Everything inside me screamed, "IT'S JUST NOT FAIR!" Then to top it off, I was losing my left breast due to a clerical error! Are you kidding me? I told Jesus on them all!!! It wasn't my fault, yet I would be the one to pay for it with a body part.

FOOTPRINTS

Do you remember the print and verse FOOTPRINTS? I had just bought it and hung it up before all this happened. I now envisioned myself seeing Jesus on the beach…just a few hundred feet away. He was already on His way to me. I ran to Him bawling my head off and screaming "Jesus, I have cancer!" I jumped into His open and welcoming arms, buried my head in His chest wailing, "I can't do this alone, Jesus. I just can't." He just comforted me with His shushing voice rocking me side to side. I knew I wouldn't be alone. Ever! He promised. From then on I was able to fixate on moving forward doing all I could to meet this monster with all the positive mindedness I could muster. Jesus took care of the rest down to the minute detail.

TIME FOR RESEARCH

While waiting for my surgery date to arrive, I busied myself researching and studying all I could on the breast. I read a 600-page book on Breast Health and Diseases. The option I chose was to have my lump removed surgically. My homework was completed. Now it was time to wait until time for my surgery. How blessed I am to have siblings that decided we needed to all be together before my surgery. We camped as an extended family for the 6th time that year. Many pictures were taken. It was, of course, a delightful and encouraging family time. My Mom and Sister came the night before surgery. During that evening, my husband decided I should not have surgery at all, but rather try a new medical 'cure for all cancers'. I told him I had made a studied decision to have my tumor surgically removed. What a rough night! My husband was upset because I chose to have surgery. Did I make the right choice for all of us?

TIME FOR SURGERY

All the forms are signed. All kisses have been given and received. It turned out my tumor was not one lump. It was not even two. It was a U-shaped tumor that lay on my ribs and must all come out. I went in for a lumpectomy and came out with a radical mastectomy. All my breast tissue and 22 lymph nodes were removed. None of the lymph nodes were cancerous. How blessed I was to have a type of cancer you can remove and sit on a counter! Yes, I had signed forms for the surgeon to do what was minimal but best for my longevity. Now it's time for healing up completely. Remember I had mentioned my surgery date was the day before my forty-fifth birthday? My nurses came in at midnight with a cake and a lit candle singing happy birthday! Then they took out my I.V.! What a 45th birthday gift. How very thoughtful!

CANCER TREATMENTS BEGIN

After three months of healing, it's time to begin my six intravenous chemotherapy treatments followed by radiation. Upon starting my chemotherapy treatments, they informed me my white blood cell counts were very low. I had the throwing up and nausea feelings from my chemotherapy, but what plagued me most was my fatigue. At church people didn't complain about me lying down while Kevin preached. One particular day, I was walking from the kitchen to the couch in the front room only because I knew I couldn't make it down the hall to my bed. As it turned out, I couldn't make it to the couch. I lay down on the floor and asked for a pillow and a blanket. My 13-year-old daughter, Cora, and 15-year-old son Samuel quickly grabbed both and came back to 'tuck me in' right there on the floor. Jonathan, my 16-year-old son on the other hand, ran straight to the phone and called Daddy. Kevin not only came home immediately, he burst through the door. It was many years later Jonathan told me he had called Daddy because he thought I was dying.

NO HAIR FOR MY HAIRBRUSH

Yes, that day finally came at the beginning of my second round of chemotherapy. When I got out of bed, it looked like a body tape line was all around where I had slept. All my body hair just came off in the night. As I showered, my hair came out by the handfuls. I knew it was coming. My scalp had ached for days prior. I called for Kevin and asked him to bring in the children one at a time, so they could see the amount of hair on the side of the tub, hoping this would be less of a shock when they saw me. The wig was too tight. My turbans hurt my head. I wore them to church for the benefit of others. As soon as I came through the door, off they came.

After both my third and fourth chemotherapy sessions, I was admitted to the hospital with a fever. Cora stayed with me every minute. The doctor made sure I was pumped full of antibiotics. Cora slept in a fold out stuffed chair that made into a twin-sized bed. Several times the nurses tried to convince her she should eat in the cafeteria and maybe go for a walk outside. She wouldn't hear of it! Off she'd go to grab her meal and beat feet to get back to me. I'll mention here how I had prayed. I didn't pray for my survival. (This really upset my Mom. Of course, she told me she prayed for my complete healing and she would never stop.) I prayed for God's will to be done. I prayed what was best for the Kingdom to come about. He is the Potter and God needed me to just stay clay. So instead of "Why Me?" I thought "Why not me?" I knew for an absolute fact God would turn this into something good. Well, there was one other thing I prayed…not to die in front of my children. This was never mentioned to anyone else. Did Cora know somehow? It was much later that the nurses told me they tried to keep Cora out of my room as much as possible. Why? The results of all my tests all pointed to imminent death.

JUST FOR JULIA

My God and my King performed a miracle that was tailor made just for me! Earlier, I told you of my medical background. So here it is. My white blood cell count was the lowest I had ever seen in my laboratory findings that survived! While working in the Hematology department of the Laboratory I had seen numerous low blood counts. But, by the time I called the doctor with the results of these patients, they had already died. God did not slide this miracle under the door. It was an obvious "Just for Julia" miracle! Now with my white blood cell count so low, it was dangerous for me to stay in the hospital. They sent me home immediately with no visitors. My doctor told me that was my last

Intravenous chemotherapy treatment. And all radiation treatments had been canceled. Oral chemotherapy continued for the next five years. My three children became my 'junk yard dogs'! No one was allowed to enter our house!

BLESSINGS GALORE

Kevin had preached several places all over the country. Cards of encouragement came in from literally everywhere! Today I still have three popcorn tins full of cards. I was overwhelmed by not only the response of the relationships worldwide, but our local congregation just could not stop helping in one way or another. One couple came before I even had surgery and asked what I needed. I told them I needed a swing for my daughter in the front yard and a tub handrail. The men of the congregation busied themselves making a swing. Women brought in meals for weeks and weeks. One sweet sister from church came over and told me to get out of bed! She changed the sheets for me. There couldn't have been a better gift. Other men and women came and washed the dishes. I now understood firsthand what the Bible verse in Philippians 4:7 meant when it said, *"And the peace of God that transcends all understanding, will guard your hearts and your minds in Christ Jesus."* There was no experience like that! Other blessings include my Aunt Retha who finally went to have her first mammogram. She also was diagnosed with breast cancer. It was in its early stages. They started right away on treatments for her which extended her life. That alone was worth it all. But there is more! Kevin had preached a funeral for a member of the congregation. When the funeral was over, we went to visit another member of the congregation who had just been diagnosed with pancreatic cancer. This sweet man was still in an anger stage upon hearing of his diagnosis. He was ranting on to us and his family when he screamed, "No one knows what I'm going through." I pulled off my turban, exposing my bald head. Now we were both sitting there – bald. Not a word was spoken. The room cleared leaving just the two of us there together – holding hands and crying. If for no other reason, I knew I was bald "for such a time as this." God used me to help this man and it felt great! What a blessing to be part of God's plan to minister to another!

AND THERE'S MORE

The unity our family experienced through this whole time period was cementing for certain. To lighten our dismal times, I took off my turban and allowed my children to take pictures of me while I made faces. We'd laugh our heads off! They did so many little things for me. I have a love of crunching leaves. My children giggled as they ran and gathered leaves to bring to the porch during my weakest times, just so I could crunch the leaves. What sweet, sweet memories. One of my most priceless pictures is the five of us in my turbans. Samuel refers to that picture as the year "we" had cancer. How profound was that?! Cancer doesn't affect one member of a family. It affects all of us. Throughout their teenage years they never shied away from holding my hand in public, giving each other kisses and other public displays of affection. They knew how close we came to not being together. To this very day, nineteen years later and still cancer free, my adult children still hold my hand.

LESSONS LEARNED

1. You are responsible for your own healthcare. Once you receive the results from the Doctors office, call to confirm the diagnosis with the Radiology Department. You must do it in that order. The Radiology Department is not allowed to give you the results of your mammogram. They send your test results to the doctor, and then the doctor's office tells you.

2. Leave notes and questions for the Doctor's Nurse, not the Doctor. This works more efficiently and effectively. Do not leave a message for the Nurse more than once. This slows her down.

3. Instead of waiting until my hair falls out on its own, I would shave my head.

4. Now that I've had I.V. chemotherapy treatments, I will not ever chastise anyone for choosing not to go through chemotherapy. You do not know what you are asking them to suffer.

5. Each person in the family has their own way of coping. Do not require more than they can do nor try to change their behavior. Cora wouldn't leave my side for a minute. She clearly remembers every detail. Samuel and Jonathan, though very helpful, have little memory of that time period. This applies not only to things surrounding my cancer, but other areas as well. Kevin stayed at the office. They EACH did the best they could.

6. Last and most important of all, God is in control! Thank Him for every breath you breathe. Enjoy each moment of the day. Stop and praise Him for all He has done and will do for you. THIS IS NOT HEAVEN. Jesus had trouble on Earth and so will we until we get Home Forever in Heaven. I can honestly say, fifteen years later, that experiencing and surviving cancer has undoubtedly been one of the biggest blessings of my life!

Our Scars Of Hope

Chapter 5

The Scars of Alcoholism

At 6 years old, even with a pillow over my head, I could hear the loud voices of my parents arguing downstairs. I hated this part of the night, when they'd return home from the bar or bowling alley, my dad drunk, abusing each other with their words. Sometimes when I couldn't stand it anymore, with tears in my eyes I'd go downstairs yelling over them to "Shut up! Stop!" Of course, it never did anything but avert their anger from one another to me, so I'd go back upstairs, lay in bed waiting for all to be quiet again.

Growing up with four siblings, an alcoholic father, a mother who waitressed at night and became a mom so young she didn't really know how to be a mother, was my normal. Our family life was the combination of my parent's upbringing. Although my paternal grandmother was a Christian, my dad's father was an alcoholic as were most of his eleven siblings. My mom, also from a family of 13 grew up in the poorer area of Tennessee, when teen marriage was expected.

As a child I always seemed to respond to the turmoil at home differently than my siblings. They were able to harden their hearts, ignore it by doing their own thing, causing trouble at school, running wild in the neighborhood, arguing among themselves, even drinking, smoking, doing drugs, and becoming sexually active at young ages. On the other hand, my heart remained soft. I tried to keep the peace any way possible. I did my chores, hated breaking rules, studied hard and avoided arguing, all reasons my siblings dubbed me 'goody two shoes'. I really thought if all of us kids were good, our dad wouldn't have any reason to be angry or drink, and our mom would want to stay home more, resulting in a normal fun family life.

At seven years old, as a means to get out of the house, I started attending church with a neighborhood friend, whose dad was the pastor. I remember enjoying the quietness of the church even though it was filled with people and wishing our family was one of those in attendance. About a year after I began attending church, our teacher in Children's Church asked those who wanted to accept Jesus into their hearts to walk forward, and I responded. And although there were many times I didn't obey Him or walk close by him, I believe that decision helped protect me from becoming self-destructive while living in a family of alcoholism, lying, self-loathing, anger, unfaithfulness and divorce.

Throughout elementary and middle school I attended the church becoming very involved in children's choir, and Pioneer Girls (similar to Girl Scouts). Because my parents had no interest, the church bus picked me up for Sunday school. I walked to any other activities I wanted to attend. All of which was okay with me as long as I was able to get out of the house.

Until I was thirteen the routine around our house was pretty much the same, my parents gone in the evenings, dad working days, my mom sleeping in, rarely getting up to see us off to school, evenings and weekends me retreating to my bedroom to avoid everyone else in the family, my siblings running wild, and punishment for all of us when someone got caught doing something wrong at home or school.

We were rarely praised for doing something right, shown outward affection, or told, "I love you". Even family dinners, served at exactly 5:30, were stressful. Not laughing or reminiscing about the good stuff in our days, but arguing, criticizing, or silence.

My parent's jobs were steady, but not high paying, so with the drinking, money was always an issue bringing about its own set of problems with a family of seven. Celebrations like Christmas was very low key, birthdays were usually just another day, family outings were rare, and clothes were usually hand-me-downs. Resulting in my feeling inferior, not important, hiding who I really was or wanted to be.

In spite of our tumultuous home life, I loved my parents. When I was 13 they divorced. It definitely wasn't a surprise, but it devastated me emotionally. Yes, we moved, yes the house was quieter, but it still didn't feel like a home, because nothing had changed in how my parents were living their lives, only now they were doing it separately putting us kids in the middle. During this change I stopped attending church, I'm not sure now if it was because I was embarrassed to ride the Sunday School bus as a teen, I lost interest, or I didn't want others to know about my life, regardless I lost touch with God, although He never left me.

During my freshman year of high school through a series of events, including something very tragic, my parents reconciled, and to avoid small town gossip about all that had occurred we moved about 25 miles away. Obviously, this meant I had to transfer schools in the middle of a semester.

By this time I was extremely insecure, ashamed of my family, had a very low self-image, and felt utterly empty inside. Like any teen I wanted to be loved, accepted, have real friends, and enjoy life. Yet I was living in a place where I knew no one. In the new school everyone had grown up together, I was an outsider. However, I did have one friend from my hometown whose family attended a church halfway between the two towns. It had a bus that would pick me up each Sunday. So out of a desperate need to be around a friend, I began taking the bus to church again. I eventually became very involved in the youth group and choir. I must admit it wasn't my extreme love for the Lord that pushed me to attend, but the need to be away from our house, to be around people that seemed normal and the search for acceptance.

During this time I began to live three lives. One at home, one at the new school where I was trying to fit in, and another at church where I personified the 'perfect well-adjusted teen'. Wherever I was I tried to be what I thought the group I was with would want me to be, for that reason I never really got close to anyone because I knew they didn't know the real me. In fact, neither did I.

My triple life continued throughout the last three years of high school. Since my parents required me to work to pay for my own clothes, get a car, and to have any spending money, I didn't have time to be involved in extracurricular activities at school or church that would help build friendships. I never really fit in with the 'jocks', and although I felt I should fit in with the 'hoods' and I did hang out with them occasionally, I didn't want to fit in with them. With the problems at home escalating in every area, including teen pregnancies, arrests, etc., I was embarrassed by it all, so I rarely talked about myself. When I was invited to someone's home, I inwardly compared my life with those families, resulting in more shame and the feeling of not being good enough which made making true friends impossible.

After high school graduation I had no direction for my life. Although I had been accepted to several colleges, my parents, assuming I'd end up being a young single mom on welfare like my sisters, insisted it would just be a waste of time and money. This was hard as I always dreamed of being a teacher, but by this time in my life, I started to believe I really wouldn't amount to anything. I wasn't sure God really did have a good plan for me.

My parents had once again divorced; my self-worth was at an all-time low, I had almost immediately lost contact with high school friends, most of who were going off to college, so that summer church became my lifeline. The pastor for the college age group suggested I attend a trip to the Boundary Waters with the group, so I did. That trip is where I started to see God's plan for my life. After roughing it for seven days which included no electricity, toilets, carrying a canoe, eating dehydrated food, sleeping in tents and visits from bears, with the same group of people a bond developed along with the beginning of feeling accepted for being me. I also met an amazing Christian, whom I married just eleven months later. Without a positive example of a healthy marriage I wasn't sure what I was doing, but I plunged in headfirst because of the unconditional love I felt from him.

In the midst of our own crazy chaos, having four kids in less than six years, I steered clear of all the chaos in the lives of my extended family. I focused on doing all I could, NOT to be like any of them. To put that life behind me, I strove to create with my children the life I always longed for as a child by becoming the perfect godly Proverbs 31 wife and mom. I worked at becoming Miss Happy Homemaker, June Cleaver, the creator of the blissful household. We raised our children to love God, one another and others, to be honest, kind, and responsible. We served in various areas at church, led a couples Bible study and I was involved in a young mom's group. I cooked homemade meals, decorated our house on a budget, home-schooled, sewed most of our three girls' clothes, and became involved in all their activities. I did all of this out of deep love for my family, but I also knew in my heart I was trying to prove to myself and others I wasn't as insecure as I felt inside.

For years I talked to my parents only occasionally. Since I didn't want our kids exposed to the realities of alcoholism, we didn't see them or my siblings very often. Both of my parents had married other people, my dad continued to drink, and my mom never really showed any interest in my life or the lives of her grandchildren. I knew they all thought I felt I was too good for them, and although I did love them all, I told myself I was protecting our children and according to the Bible we shouldn't associate with the ungodly. I also hated the reminder of the life I had as a child.

It wasn't until after my brother's unexpected death at the age of 36 when my dad hit rock bottom that my attitude began to change. My dad was living in squalor with an alcoholic wife drinking himself to death. Although he was only 59, he was suffering from severe cirrhosis of the liver. The doctor gave him just a few weeks to live. After discussion and prayer, we decided to see if he'd move in with us for what we assumed would be his final days. He agreed and stopped drinking alcohol cold turkey, which to this day I feel is a miracle. I followed the doctor's no sodium diet for him and although his cirrhosis remains, his health improved dramatically. In fact, he not only celebrated his 60th birthday while living with us, he is now doing great at 82 years old.

I always wanted to be a daddy's girl, so even though it was an added responsibility to my already full load, I enjoyed having him live with us. It was during the seven months he lived with us before getting his own apartment that I started to see him differently, see him as God wanted me to see him, not perfect, but my dad. The dad God had chosen for me. Those months of close contact with my dad helped me develop a better, yet still reserved relationship with my parents and siblings.

It's been more than twenty years since my dad lived with us; life has had its ups and downs, twists and turns, especially with my extended family. My upbringing created in me a deep hole to feel, a true sense of emptiness. Even as an adult I continued to try to do all the right things so people would like me. I became a people pleaser. With my low self-esteem I had a hard time showing affection, never really feeling I was good enough. I learned not to expect much from others knowing it would only lead to disappointment and suffered an extreme fear of rejection always worried I'd do or say something stupid, yet, God has always been faithful.

As time passed, I've been able to see how God intervened throughout my life in spite of my situations. He placed a pastor with a daughter my age in our neighborhood knowing I'd attend church with them. After my acceptance of Him as my Savior, I had convictions. At the time I thought I was just afraid get into trouble, to smoke, drink, stay out late, skip school, etc....but I now know God placed those convictions on my heart to protect me. Even the many times, especially in my teen years, when I didn't make the right decisions, when I was trying to do whatever it took to gain the approval of others, to be loved, He protected me. At church activities I memorized scriptures, never realizing at the time how they'd remain with me to give me strength. He placed godly women in my life with healthy marriages, to exemplify love, to mentor me, including my mother-in-law. When we moved, and I was so alone, He led me to the church my friend attended where I recommitted my life to Him, got baptized, met my husband, married and began raising our four kids.

God also restored and allowed me to fulfill many of my dreams. After not being able to attend college, I thought my desire to become a teacher and writer was over, however God gave me the opportunity to home school our children, something I had never thought of doing. To be able to open the world up to my children through educating them was a greater fulfillment of my dream than I could've ever imagined. Then after our kids were adults, He opened the doors to writing opportunities, (including this one) allowing me to encourage other women.

God has protected me mentally, by not allowing my heart to become hard, cold and unable to love. On the contrary, the opposite has happened. I love freely, in a way I was never taught as a child, by accepting others as they are. I've learned without Christ in their lives, others love in the way they were taught or experienced love. My parents loved the best they knew how, and although I wanted more, it would be wrong to judge them or hold

48

bitterness in my heart toward them, which allows me to have the good relationship I have with them now. God's love has shown me we are all imperfect people who are infinitely, perfectly loved.

The most important way God intervened in my life was to be available, to pick me up when I was down, to forgive my mistakes, to show me I was worthy, loveable, and valuable. Even now although my relationship with the Lord has grown and I know He loves me unconditionally, there are times I still struggle with not being good enough for Him or others. When those moments happen, I search my heart for the verses I memorized as a child, or look around me at the multitude of blessings in my life. After all, if I was worthless I'm sure the God of the Universe wouldn't take the time to fill my life with an abundance of blessings, including a loving marriage of 38 years and counting, amazing children, genuine friendships, adorable grandchildren, a good relationship with my parents and siblings, a home, fulfillment of dreams, and the opportunity to be who he created me to be.

The scars caused by my father's alcoholism will always be part of who I am, causing occasional feelings of being insecure, unworthy, unlikeable, inferior, and a failure. However, just as the pain of those years won't be forgotten my Heavenly Father is faithful to continually apply the balm of His love to soothe the painful memories, as He covers the scars with His hands that have the scars of nails, His cost of love, reminding me of the sacrifice He made not to harm me, but to bring me hope and a future. (Jeremiah 29:11).

Chapter 6

Ears to Hear

One time, before my Mom went home to be with the Lord, she shared a story with me about when I was little. She said she saw gray mist around me when I was 6 weeks old and she knew something was wrong. My dad was not too happy to hear her talk about seeing things. They took me to the hospital because I was screaming so terribly that my dad couldn't handle it. I was so sick with a bile blocked duct that I almost died. The medicine Gentamicin kept me alive, but later we found out that it also caused my deafness. The doctors didn't know how much to give me since I was a baby, and in large doses it's toxic.

At that time, my Mom had gone home for a short time to care for my two older sisters. But, when she went back to the hospital and saw me she grabbed my finger and she raised her hand to the Lord and said she felt electricity warm around her arm to her hand and to my body. Surprisingly, shortly afterward the doctor said that I was doing great! God healed me that day! God had a purpose for me to be alive.

When I was 16 months old I was a very happy baby. My mom kept calling my name, but I didn't turn around. Then she stomped on the floor and I felt the vibration and I turned around towards her. She thought there was something wrong with me. She said, "Rosemary". I laughed and smiled at her. She told my dad "She can't hear me"! And he said, "She turned around, so she can hear you". He was in denial about the possibility of me being deaf. She said, "No, something's wrong with her". So, they took me to the doctor and found out that I was deaf.

I went to a deaf school from age 3 to 13 to learn how to read lips and talk. But, it was my mom who really helped me learn to read lips and talk the most. Since I couldn't hear, she would use a feather in front of my mouth when she was teaching me, so I could see it move when I spoke.

I wasn't able to learn sign language at school or at home. My fifth sister (I'm the 3rd girl of 10 daughters) tried to explain to my parents that I needed to learn sign language. They refused to let me learn to sign. Even my deaf school wouldn't let me learn sign language. If they saw me moving my hands, they would put ropes around them or hit them with a ruler. I didn't understand why they didn't want me to know sign language. It made me very sad! I was a straight 'A' student until I entered high school. School became overwhelming for me because I didn't know sign language. I could only read lips. I had difficulty talking with other deaf people.

My two older sisters didn't want to play with me. I got really frustrated with them because I tried to join them to play and they pushed me away. They thought I was stupid! They didn't want to play with me and told me to go away. It was hard because I felt alone. I decided to try to be more independent. I helped my Mom care for my seven younger sisters. I walked with them to school and sometimes played with them after school.

I was a happy girl until I was 9 years old. A couple of my younger sisters and I went over to visit our neighbor couple next door. They weren't allowed to go by themselves since they were little. The man would take me downstairs to the basement and molest me. My sisters were busy talking to his wife who was blind that they weren't concerned about where I was. I thought it was okay for him to touch me at first because he said it was alright, but deep down I felt strange, even though he gave me candy each time. He always took me, never any of my sisters downstairs. Was I to feel special that he chose me to abuse sexually for several years? My sisters wanted me to go with them next door almost daily, so they could visit with his wife. I couldn't explain why I didn't want to go, so they always talked me into taking them. I became quieter than I usually was, but at the time I didn't even understand why.

When I was in health class in high school, I learned about the facts of life. It hit me hard when I finally realized that what the neighbor had been doing to me for several years was wrong. I didn't know what to do about it. I started running away and hiding, so he couldn't find me at home. I would hide in the dog house or in the back seat of our car and sometimes, I would fall asleep there. My Dad drank sometimes and when he would find me hiding, he

52

would be angry and use a belt to my back that left bruises. My Mom stood there and watched, but never stopped him from hurting me. Although, years later she apologized for not stopping him. My parents had a hard time with me because of my frustrations and anger. It was hard to communicate to them how I was feeling. I knew that they loved me and did what they thought was best for me. I didn't want to tell them about the neighbor man because I was afraid I'd get in trouble. I was ashamed of myself for letting him touch me and taking his candy for years. I finally told my older sister. I didn't know at the time that she told my Mom. Shortly afterward when I was 15, we moved away. I was so happy that I never had to see that man again!

The next summer, I met a boy at the carnival who wouldn't leave me alone! I knew that he liked me, but I didn't like him much. I would try to hide from him, hoping he would go away. I wasn't attracted to him at first, but when I saw him the next year, I thought he was so handsome. Unfortunately, I got pregnant when I was 17 years old. I was forced to marry him for "religious" reasons. I didn't love him, but that didn't seem to matter because we had to obey our parents and get married.

We lived with his parents. I wasn't very happy living there! I was overwhelmed by his parents controlling me. They refused to let me see my family for nine years. One time when my parents came to visit me, my husband wouldn't let them in and he pushed my Mom off of the porch. I was scared and didn't know what to do. I was filled with anger and bitterness! I enjoyed getting out of the house, and since they were 'religious people', I went to church with them. Little did they know that I enjoyed going to church.

By the time I was 21, I had two children, and I also had miscarried a baby girl. At that time my husband played in a gospel group. I saw people were praising the Lord with their hands. I was puzzled and didn't know why they were raising their hands in the air. I asked my friend what they were doing. She explained to me about the Lord. On my drive home I looked up to the sky and asked God, "Where are you"? When I got home, I went down to the basement alone. I saw a Bible lying on the sofa. I read it for three days without caring about food and drink. I saw a shining, bright light come out of the ceiling and saw Jesus' feet. It was so beautiful! I asked Jesus into my heart that night.

When my youngest son was born a couple of years later, I told my husband I wanted to go visit my parents. I didn't even have a driver's license at the time, so I didn't know how I was going to see them. I knew he wasn't going to drive me because he was trying to keep me away from my parents, so I began studying the driving manual myself. It took me more than a year of begging and pleading with him until he agreed to let me go. I tested for my driver's license and passed it! Finally, he let me drive over eight hours to visit my family. When I arrived I saw my mom running towards me. I ran to her and hugged her. I cried happy tears and asked her, "Mommy, why didn't you come to visit me or write me?" She said, "I did. I wrote you every day?" I said, "What? I never received them!" When I went back home, I asked my husband about the letters and he said, "I don't know what you are talking about"! One day, when I was cleaning the house I finally found a drawer full of letters that my Mom had sent me. I wept and wept when I read them. I was angry and confronted him for lying to me and asked him "Why"? He said, "Your family is bad! You don't need them!" I said, "No they are full of love. You can't judge my family because you don't even know them!" He hit me for talking to him like that. I cowered to him and went to the other room.

When I was in the hospital to have back surgery, he ignored me for five days. I didn't know if he was going to pick me up to take me home or not. That is when I had my first panic attack. When I saw him and asked him why he hadn't even called to check on me, he yelled at me and called me stupid, along with some other nasty names. I needed someone to help take care of me when I got home, but I had no one. But, I still had to care for our three boys. I was hurting and felt so alone and unloved, even by my husband.

I fell in love with sign language when I visited a church that had a sign language interpreter. It made me want to learn it. I told my husband that I wanted to go to that church, but he refused to let me go. I was hurting and talked to God and told Him that I wanted to learn sign language. Not long after we went to a restaurant, and I met a Pastor of a Deaf Ministry. I was shocked to hear the Pastor when she asked me if I was deaf. I said, "Yeah". She signed to me, but I told her that I didn't know any sign language. She continued signing, and I read her lips. I looked around for my husband and was scared that he would see us talking. When we got into the car, my husband was full of anger and he yelled at me and said that I didn't need to know sign language. When we got home, he called my parents and told them who I had met and he told them sign language is bad and he wasn't going to allow me to learn it! I wondered why no one asked me what I wanted or needed. How come I didn't matter? I continued to pray and asked God to help me learn sign language.

A short time had passed when I received a letter from a Pastor in the next state telling me about a deaf church not too far away from me. I was full of excitement! I visited there without telling my husband. If I would've asked, he wouldn't have allowed it. I met the Pastor, and he signed to me. I said, "I don't know sign language." He realized that I could read lips. He introduced me to his daughter who is deaf. She is the one who taught me to use sign language. I was thankful that God had heard my prayer.

I didn't realize it at the time, but my husband was having an affair. He told me to move out! I was shocked! But, mostly I was very hurt because I had to leave my children with him. I wasn't allowed to bring them with me. I stayed with my sweet friend for few months. I had really bad panic attacks when he pushed me away more and more and I really missed my children! They would think that I didn't love them and that I wanted to leave them. I knew that he would say mean things about me to them. I was so confused about what to do. I was hurting so much and I felt hopeless! I didn't know what to do. He eventually divorced me for another woman.

I had tried to hurt myself a few times because I couldn't find hope, love or happiness. One night I was carrying a medicine pill bottle in my hand and a voice inside said, "Look at yourself! You hate your life! Just end it now!" I was surprised when I was suddenly shaken out of my self-loathing at 2:00 in the morning, by a phone call. I was puzzled when I looked at the caller ID box and realized it was the phone number of my counselor. He said, "I felt something that woke me up and I called you". He asked me, "What do you have in your hand?" I said, "Huh"? He said, "Hmm, come into the office first thing in the morning." I agreed to be there when it opened. When I saw the counselor, I wasn't able to share my heart with him because I was scared and I didn't trust him. But, after two months I asked him, "How did he know to call me at 2:00 AM"? He said, "The Lord told me". I was surprised by his response. I was in tears when I realized that God had stopped me from killing myself by having my counselor call me. I had the reassurance that He loved me even if I felt like no one else did. It was a major turning point for me because I knew that I could finally trust someone. I shared with him a lot of things from that point on. I felt better than I had, but I was still uneasy and knew that I still had more work to do on myself. I was still searching for something more in my life.

After I'd been divorced for a few years and had learned sign language, I brought my good friend, who is a deaf interpreter with me to visit my family. We all sat together, but I couldn't read their lips because there were so many of us and they talked too fast. They were talking at the same time and it was hard for me to read all of their lips. I tried to catch up, but I couldn't. I stopped them and went upstairs and asked my friend to come down to help me communicate with my sisters. She and I sat in the middle with my sisters circling around us. I asked her to turn her voice off and for us to use sign language only. We signed for a few minutes and laughed with one another. One of my sisters said, "What did you say? It's not fair because we don't know what you're saying!" Since we weren't using our lips, they couldn't understand what we were saying to one another. "I couldn't read your lips because you talked too fast," I said. "Now you know how I felt left out of the conversation for so many years? I said, "It was not fair for me also!" My dad was standing there watching, and he finally saw the value of sign language and told them that I was right. My sisters learned a good lesson that day. And, ever since, we've become so close and shared and laughed together.

I met a lady that went through a lot in her life like I did…sexual, physical, emotional and verbal abuse…it was horrible! I thought the abuse from my husband was normal until she shared her experience with me. I was abused and scared for most of my life, and now it was beginning to make sense to me. It really hit me hard when I realized that it wasn't normal!

I searched for a church for two years and I finally found one that I liked. I was surprised to hear the pastor speak about forgiveness in his sermon. I asked myself if I still had bitterness and I asked God to give me understanding. I realized that I had a lot of forgiving to do of those who had hurt me throughout my life. And, the hurting caused by my ex-husband wasn't over. He had turned our boys against me! Most of the time they didn't want to speak to me unless they needed something. I wondered what lies he had told them about me.

I was puzzled about forgiveness. I'd been hurt by people that were supposed to love and protect me. How do I forgive them? When I heard the sermon about what the Lord had done for me by dying on the cross and forgiving my sins, I knew I had to forgive, but I didn't know how. I bowed down on the floor before the Lord and cried for what seemed like hours, until the pastor came to me and told me, "Let it go!" I said, "What?" He said, "God told me to tell you to let it go!" I said, "OK" and I ran to the altar and wept.

The Pastor's wife met with me and taught me more about forgiveness. I shared my story with her. I cried so much! She gave me big, huge hugs that made me feel loved! And, once again I saw myself as the young girl who was so happy. I realized who I was. I felt different, but better, once I learned how to forgive. I had been so full of anger and bitterness for such a very long time! It was beautiful how the Lord had helped me!

I struggled and searched for years to know real love. I finally found love with a new husband. He is so good at caring for me and he makes me feel so safe, especially when he hugs me. God has blessed me with a loving husband that treats me better than I've ever been treated in my life. I am so thankful for the seven years we've been together!

I also found love at the church that I now attend. The Pastor and his wife have been through so much in their lives, and have experienced His love and forgiveness themselves, that they willingly share it with others. I immediately saw God's beautiful love and support in them. They've encouraged me a lot!

One day I was curious and wanted to see what the children's teacher was teaching the children. As I watched their little faces, I started to pick up many things from them, and somehow I saw love at work right there. The little kids were full of laughter and love and many things I find difficult to explain. I guess it was their innocence that stood out to me. I remembered I had been a happy little girl once. Then I was asked me if I wanted to teach kids. I was shocked and thrilled at the same time because I had been a ladies deaf class teacher for 15 years at a former church. I asked her, "How did you know"? It hit me hard because I knew it was from God. He has now called me to teach children.

Since then, I've been learning more about the love of God through the children. I am so thankful for God's love and for Him opening my eyes to see many things. I'm also excited to be a part of the women's ministry and to see the love of God shared among all the women. There's nothing like being accepted and loved by them.

I pray that my story touches your heart and that you'll learn as I did, that God loves you very much! Deafness has made my life challenging, and some have taken advantage of what they saw as a weakness in me, but God has used it to show His mercy and love, as I've forgiven them. I have chosen to accept my deafness and move on to what God wants me to do. I've realized that God is using my wounded experiences to help others. I will continue to be an overcomer because He has given me eyes to see what good He can do in my life, and a heart to share His love with others. I may not be able to hear you, but when I listen, I can hear what God is telling me to do. Can you hear Him?

"He who has ears to hear, let him hear." Matthew 3:9

Chapter 7

Fitting In...Or Not

Well, I've put off writing this. I wonder why? I think it is because as I look back over 60 plus years, I wish I had done better. And yet, I know at each step I really was working at it and felt I did the best I could. So, what has been the challenge I've dealt with: How to feel like I fit into my "in-law" family when our family styles turned out to be pretty different. And basically, we are talking mother-in-law. I count my blessings in so many ways and feel some guilt that this has even been an issue in my life...but it has. The hurt I felt was very real at times. Maybe others can learn from my experience and do better. I hope so.

Listen, here's the deal: The paradigm from which we come is going to be what feels normal to us—not perfect—just normal. So, I moved into my husband's "land", his territory. And I love his family and I wanted to be a part of it. And I was...except over the years it became obvious to me that I just didn't think like they did because I came from a different background. I was raised to be very independent, trusted with lots of responsibility, expected to handle things, value discussions and differences of opinions, embrace adventure and take on the changes of the world. Then I entered "Safe-ville"...where the girls went to the store two by two...what??? The doors were locked soundly always...I mean always. Be suspicious. The world was not to be trusted. Keep things the same (in fact, can we just return to the 1950s?), embrace Leave It to Beaver World. Your own comfort is number one in this world. And apparently, cleanliness is next to godliness—OCD style. Forget bargains and coupons...get what you want especially if it is food. Don't cut corners there. And dinners were perfect. And on time. And had dessert. It felt unusual to me for sure. I was a farm girl, and we pulled off dinner at 9 pm sometimes after working outside with the animals until there was no more light.

59

And I loved the craziness of my world. Relationships, not food and cleaning, were what we did. So, I began realizing I was the odd duck in this territory for sure. And, they liked me just fine---I went with the flow.

So, why did it feel hard? Again, good question looking back. I'm sure I was too sensitive in wanting to feel like I fit. I wish I had done better. Been more understanding. But it takes time to "get it" and now in my mid-60s I think I do. But when I had young children and needed help from a mother-in-law to watch kids while one of mine had surgery, and she told me she couldn't because she was going somewhere with one of the daughters that day…well, that was devastating. I never asked for babysitting help…and it wasn't volunteered. It was several little things like that, which I know she didn't do to hurt me…she just ONLY pictures the world of her OWN children first. Especially the girls…and there were three. There really is no need for a daughter-in-law when you have three daughters of your own. And they are all very, very, very nurturing—very co-dependent. It wears me out to see how they worry and stew over each other. Or maybe I just feel left out. They worry over everything. If all is going well, they dream up some "what-if" to worry over. It's exhausting. Input I have really is not ever desired. They all have the "perfect" ways to do whatever-the right way-their way. They cook perfect. They clean perfect-they clean a lot. They peel potatoes perfect (as I discovered when my mother-in-law re-peeled them when I got done. Sigh. "I must be an idiot," I say to myself.) I never knew it was important to do so many things so perfectly. Somehow, I could never even think about washing dishes in such excessively thorough ways. And yet I wanted to fit in so much. And they liked me….but I knew I didn't do the "perfect" like they did. And I didn't really want to be like that. But, I did want to feel like I fit in. It was like I had moved to a foreign land.

So, I would turn to my husband and explain my thoughts and he would comfort me and make me feel better. Hmmm….not quite. He meant well, but even though he never said it, it was apparent his family's ways were the "right" ways of course. He could never see the issue with things his mother said to me that hurt….such as when I called and invited her and grandpa to dinner. And she said,

"I'll need to ask *** (one of the daughters) first. Why? I had invited them. I wanted them to come over. I was excited. I felt shot down. It felt as if she needed to make sure there was nothing the girls needed her to do…because that is the priority (it seemed to say to me).

As I look back, over the many hurt moments that tended to happen a lot, I realize she is a nice lady who has no friends outside her children (who all adore her), and really only seeks her children (mostly), and her husband (some) to be part of her world. The rest of us she likes…but we are second tier. The other daughter-in-law lives in a different state and I guess I should take heart knowing the two of them barely can speak and have had some bad run-ins over the years, because of the way my mother-in-law coddles her younger son. No wife wants to see that. My husband is the older son and won't stand for being coddled. So, I guess all in all…as daughter-in-law's go, she thinks I'm fine. And I do feel good that over the years, where it has hurt me, I have not spoken back in a way to cause any trouble in the family. So, nobody really knows my hurts but my spouse, and bless his heart, he just can't see that it is an issue. He has never been able to say, "I love the way you do things. I love the way you help others. I love the way you teach the children at church. I love that you care enough for others to go on mission trips. I love that you cook and clean for us, but you do it for others too." His norm was a mom who just tended to her own family. Why would I do all of that other stuff??

And I guess, because of needing and wanting reassurance and not hearing it, I was left to assume that his mother (who did not do those things because she was always just cooking and cleaning for the family) was the ideal to live up to and I fell short of that. I think my mother-in-law is a lovely version of "herself", but I do not seek to be someone who only does for her own family. I just can't be that. I don't want to be that. I think God has given me opportunities to do other things too. Don't get me wrong. I loved cleaning and cooking and tending to my family. I spent lots of time doing it. I just felt like I had time to serve others too. Is this making sense? I think both of us are fine—just different, very different. So here I am, surrounded by his family, his family's ways, and his family's territory. And I've got some empty inside me because I just don't feel like I measure up and fit in.

Sometimes, it really does feel like I have been planted in a foreign world. I think really, I just needed someone to tell me I'm okay, their ways are just a bit different and that's okay. But there isn't anyone who could say that and understand. As the aging process has happened, and the ways of retirement have become apparent, I see another "very, very different" approach than my family has taken; mine tend to live strong and work hard and value being worn out at the end of the day and go adventure as long as possible, while the in-laws world shrinks to just the kids who tell them to slow down, take it easy, being tired is very, very bad...how much easier can a person take it. LIVE! But then, what do I know? And when my spouse thinks that all is well with that approach, I have stomach-churning panic thinking that he thinks we should do the same. Which he does...well, he did. Honestly, as the folks have aged more and tried to leave home as little as possible, their ideology has become more apparent to him. He finally, after 40 years of marriage acknowledged that it was probably not good. Whew! They can age in any way they desire, but please don't trap me into thinking that is the only way to do it. I think God wants us to keep shining for Him all the way home! And arrive used up!

So, I could tell more random stories, but you get the idea. I am thankful for so many things, but I do feel a hurt from this that was hard to "fix." Your situation will be a different scenario, but it might be causing you hurt and confusion. So, what can I sum up at this stage of my life that might be helpful to you at your stage?

- Be prepared to learn many things throughout life and accept that there are many "right" ways to do things. Be okay with that. You can seek to understand your situation, or you may never totally understand it. But you can have control of YOU. Don't let something else have control of you.
- Really, don't sweat the small stuff and sensitivity to things that you know aren't intended to be mean...yes, it hurts, but it is the small stuff. Be bigger. It is probably a lacking in that other person to not recognize what they have done or said—

and in me for being too sensitive to it. Most of the things done are not on purpose; I feel certain of that. It has been eye-opening as I became a mother-in-law myself, to see how easy it is to mistakenly do a mis-step. Some may deal with people who do hurtful things that ARE on purpose, but I really think for most situations, it is not on purpose when others make comments that hurt. I've concluded that our biggest enemy at times like this is in our own head when we CAN'T. LET. IT. GO. I have grasped on to

2 Corinthians 10:5b..." and *we are <u>taking every thought captive</u> to the obedience of Christ"*. Good idea. Keep those thoughts from circling our brain in an endless progression of "heading *nowhere* productivity." Life flies by pretty fast. Don't waste too many moments stewing. You are choosing to rob yourself if you do.

- It's nice if there is a sympathetic ear to understand, but even if you explain it, the person can't feel it like you can, so again, just be the bigger person. Let God be your sounding board and that is enough.
- <u>Philippians 4:6-7</u> *"Do not be anxious about anything, but in everything by prayer and supplication with thanksgiving let your requests be made known to God. And the peace of God, which surpasses all understanding, will guard your hearts and your minds in Christ Jesus"*. 1 Peter 5:7 "Casting *all your anxieties on him, because he cares for you"*.
- Embrace the Bible words of encouragement...so many speak of love. Especially writings by John. I love those! Colossians 3:14-15 is good as well. *"Beyond all these things put on love, which is the perfect bond of unity. Let the peace of Christ rule in your hearts, to which indeed you were called in one body; and be thankful"*. Embrace this!
- Fill up with gratitude. Take a moment and look around and appreciate all the good things in your situation. Focus on those more, the other things less. Colossians 3:16 *"Let the word of Christ richly dwell within you, with all wisdom teaching and admonishing one another with psalms and hymns and spiritual songs, singing with thankfulness in your hearts to God"*.

- Keep busy doing good. Nothing fixes the "dwelling on my issue" better than helping someone else.
  Hebrews 13:16 *"And do not forget to do good and to share with others"*.
  Matthew 5:16 *"In the same way let your light shine before others, that they may see your good deeds and glorify your Father in heaven"*.
  Call an elderly church member, keep a young mom's toddler while she does errands one morning, give a friendly thank you to a busy clerk in the store, make some cookies and go deliver them! I am happy to say these things have helped me be at peace. Many people deal with much more difficult issues, but if something hurts, it hurts. So process...and then take action and do what YOU can do. That is all you can really change in the end...with God's help. May God bless you as we all walk together seeking our heavenly home.

Chapter 8

Loss Of A Living Child

I was excited to see my son, Matthew, and his girlfriend, Amanda, walk into the room for an unexpected visit. Little did I know about the bombshell that was about to explode minutes later. I stood there dumbfounded as he read his letter to me. He had a sad look on his face and the paper shook as he said, "I wish this wasn't true, but from this moment on I can't see you anymore." Did he really say what I think I heard? "What? You've already cut your time with me because of Amanda. Now it's nothing?" He replied, "I wish it wasn't true, but we found out that your husband, Max, is a registered sex offender. We can't have any more contact with you because of our daughters." I glanced over at Amanda, and she stood cross armed with an evil smirk on her face that will be embedded in my mind for a very long time. "Let me explain. It's not true! He was framed by his ex-wife!" I said. They cut me off and wouldn't listen to my explanation. My tears began to flow. Matthew folded up his letter, and he and Amanda walked out of the room.

Amanda took it upon herself to tell the rest of the family about Max being a registered sex offender. She didn't waste any time calling my family and my ex-husband and anybody that would listen to her rant. Over the next few days I did damage control to explain the truth. All the people that Amanda called felt betrayed and were angry that I hadn't revealed it several years ago when I first met Max. They want to believe me, but they're having a hard time since they think that I lied to them. But I didn't lie and frankly, it's really not any of their business!

Max had been married to a lady who had two children when they wed. He had found out that she was using drugs and drinking heavily and decided to divorce her. She didn't want a divorce and threatened to ruin his life if he followed through with it. He had no idea what she meant, but it wasn't long before he found out!

Before their divorce was final, she had him arrested for 'touching' her 8-year-old daughter. She told him after he posted bail that if he came back to her, she would drop the charges. What mother would take back a man who had sexual contact with her daughter? Not any that I know! It seemed suspicious to me.

Max is a veteran and had never been in trouble with the law. He went to his trial and the Public Defender scared him into a 'guilty' plea by telling him that if he didn't plead guilty, he would go to prison for 25 years and be raped every day. Well, the idea of that was enough of a threat to make him choose the 'guilty' plea. He had no idea how this admittance of guilt would affect his life, his jobs, where he lived, his relationships, and mostly, his self-esteem the rest of his life.

When Max told me his story on our first date, I believed him. There are women that manipulate men to get what they want. His sexual offender status wasn't an issue for me until my son disowned me. Don't misunderstand me, I love my husband, but I also ache for my son. I wish that Max would've gotten legal counsel before admitting guilt years ago. Wherever he works and wherever we live, it must be approved by the city police. It's embarrassing for him and me too!

Max wouldn't hurt anyone. He's very kind hearted. He makes it a point to not be around children. When we've had grandchildren over, he's never alone with them. This is how I can help to make sure that Max never gets accused of this ever again. He's very cautious around children. I would never put my grandchildren or anyone in harm's way. My son and Amanda know that I've always been around when Max and I were watching my grandchildren. Since they've disowned me, they've had two more children. I've never been able to meet them. I've only seen them in pictures. I have four grandchildren but have mainly spent time with the oldest one. My family shares pictures and stories about them with me. When the eldest granddaughter asked to see me, she was told that "I'm no longer her Grandma." My heart breaks for not getting to spend time with my grandchildren. I don't want them to think that I don't love them. I'm angry, and extremely hurt, because I've not done anything to deserve this kind of treatment.

I don't understand how my son thinks I could do anything to hurt those precious children. For some reason, my son loves Amanda more than hearing the truth from me, his own Mother. It hurts that he's turned his back on me and threatens to file harassment charges if I text him or if a family member tries to explain the truth to him. They've tried, and he hangs up on them and tells them not to call back again or he's calling the police. I think Amanda is happy that she doesn't have to share my son with me.

I'm not angry at God, but sometimes, I find myself angry at Amanda because I believe she's the instigator of it all. I don't like feeling this way, and I'm working on my anger. I'm just so hurt and wish I could have just five minutes to explain everything to Matthew. I can understand why they don't want Max around their children but why me too? I didn't do anything! Why can't I see them? Why won't my son see me or talk to me? I've been very kind to him and Amanda. I've helped them whenever they needed help from me. She's so controlling of not just my son, but my parents and other family members. When there's a holiday, I can't be around my family, because they're going to be over. It's as if I've got leprosy or something. Why am I the outcast? My family is afraid that Amanda might keep the children away from them if I happen to show up and they're over there. How does one person have so much power? And how is it that everyone else allows it? It's very sad!

It surprises me that there are other mothers who are going through estrangement from their child. I thought I was alone but have found out about other similar situations. I don't know how long this will go on. I continue to pray that it won't be long and that I will get to spend time with my son and my grandchildren again. I've brought my son up to know Christ and pray that he will remember his youth.

Proverbs 22:6 says, *"Teach a youth about the way he should go; even when he is old, he will not depart from it." (HCSB)* This is what I hang on to and trust that God will bring healing in time. I rest in his promises. Jeremiah 29:11 says, *"For I know the plans I have for you," declares the Lord, "plans to prosper and not to harm you, plans to give you hope and a future." (NIV).*

SURVIVOR

Our status is victim but it's our choice if it stays.

We can change to survivor if we choose positive ways.

We can't change the past, it's long dead and gone.

And we're never responsible for other's choices or wrongs.

All we can do is take the cards that we're played.

Be smart, be wise, and accept God's unbelievable trade.

He offers us joy and a deep peace within.

All he asks of us, is to give our burdens to Him.

So, He can show us the beauty He makes

From the scars on our heart made by other's mistakes.

But, the best thing to see is our journey unfold,

When God uses our story as we become bold.

No longer ashamed, but empowered by truth

That we are beautiful and pure.

God's grace is the proof.

By Taylor Miller

Chapter 9

God's Providence and Provisions

My name is Lou Anne and my story's about going through four miscarriages, divorce, and God's providence. I would conceive without complications and carried my first daughter without issue during the pregnancy and delivery. I experienced four miscarriages between child number one and child number two. I learned many lessons over the years and (many times in hindsight) recognized God's providence.

One of the first lessons I realized years later was the Holy Spirit raising and waving huge red flags before I married my first husband. I loved the Lord, and he did not. I remember talking to him especially on one occasion shortly before our wedding about Christ. He was not influenced in a positive way hardly at all! To his credit, he did attend church with me for the first two years of our marriage. Our marriage was a challenge to say the least. When you don't have Christ in the center of a marriage, it will *always* be more challenging than when you both love the Lord. I was raised in the church and knew that I should not be unequally yoked to an unbeliever. He did believe in God and Christ, but they were not a priority in his life. I had sent out the invitations to the wedding and felt like I really should go ahead with the wedding because it would be such an embarrassment to call it off in the last few weeks. I was thinking it would probably work out ok. WRONG!

I had two miscarriages before seeking medical intervention. Of course, I cried buckets of tears with each one. When tested, the doctor discovered I had low progesterone levels. The babies all were lost before 11 weeks gestation because the progesterone levels did not stay high enough to sustain the pregnancy. I became pregnant again before it could be determined what levels of progesterone I needed, and the dose we tried did not work, thus a third miscarriage. With the forth miscarriage, I took a larger dose of progesterone but still lost the baby.

Finally, with pregnancy #6, the doctor recommended doubling the dose of progesterone, and I did carry that pregnancy to term. I really began seeing God's providence after that. It was around that time, my spouse took a renewed interest in playing music at bars and things like that. Our marriage grew more challenging because we had such different goals in life.

When daughter #1 was 9 years old, and daughter #2 was 18 months old, I received a phone call late at night, and the man on the phone said, "Do you know where he is going? Do you know what he is doing?" I did not recognize the voice at all. I never did find out who made that phone call. Was it an angel? I have often wondered.

My husband had a job where he had to go out at night and do testing on electrical equipment and could work into the long hours of the night, so he always had a good "reason" to be out. I completely trusted him and had no reason that I knew of, not to believe him. I immediately called his boss at work, and a coworker, and asked if they knew if he was at work that night. His boss drove to the job site and checked. He called me back to tell me that my husband was not at work. I called one of the guys in the band to ask if they were practicing music that night and they were not. He came in late that night and I did not say anything to him.

God's providence was very much at work here. I began listening to Focus on the Family in 1978. Dr. James Dobson had written a book called, *"Love Must Be Tough"*. It is most specifically written to victims of adultery. Other topics are covered too, but primarily to help those whose marriages are breaking up because of adultery. I heard him talk about it on his radio show for two or three days and thought I should order that book because I may know someone someday that may need that information. I read the book approximately one year before I received that questioning phone call. Little did I know that God was preparing *me* for *my* future, not so much for helping someone else's.

In reading Dr. Dobson's book, I learned the victim should **NEVER** beg the guilty one to stay and say they would change and do whatever the spouse wanted them to do. They should address the guilty party by saying, "you will have to choose, but you cannot have two in this relationship." The following morning, I asked him what the phone call meant. He started off with denying everything, but soon sat down, and began with, "I have been meaning to tell you..."! My world would never be the same after those words. He told me he was involved with someone else and he really cared about her. I was in total shock! God absolutely gave me the courage and recollection of what to say. Because of Dr. Dobson's book, I immediately told him that he would have to pick one of us, that I would not put up with another person in the picture. Thank you, Heavenly Father, for your providence and preparing me!

I sought council immediately with a preacher in Nashville and he stated I had done well to set boundaries. He said, "Within two to three days he will tell you an answer." Sure enough, in two or three days, he said he wanted to go. Within a week, he changed his mind again and said he wanted to stay. Not long after that, he decided he needed to leave.

At first, I was really scared thinking how on earth can I raise these two girls as a single parent and survive financially? We did go through the divorce and there was child support, which did *not* increase over the years. In hindsight, that would have been a wise provision within the divorce agreement.

My relying on the Lord grew over time. One thing I did because I was so overwhelmed originally, was to write down on a piece of paper my blessings and hang it next to my bed. I would read it aloud each morning and each evening. I called it my CYB sheet, Count Your Blessings. That really helped me not be overwhelmed by fear and doubts. Gratitude is such a vital part of healing and so important for our lives.

Another thing that proved to be absolutely necessary for my sanity was to get into God's word and read it EVERY SINGLE DAY! I had to have it for strength to get through. Someone mentioned to me that reading the Psalms was very healing. They recommended reading five chapters of Psalms per day for healing, and one chapter of Proverbs daily for wisdom. Usually three to four of the Psalms were related to the same topic, and I did find it very healing. I did that for two to three months in a row. One can begin with whatever day of the month it is to stay focused. For example: if today is June 7, 2017, begin with Psalms 7, 37, 67, 97, 127, and Proverbs 7. Keep up that 30 day succession.

Did I ever forgive him of the adultery? Yes, but it took years unfortunately. I was the main person I was hurting by the lack of forgiveness. A scripture I realized to be absolutely true was Romans 8:28, *"All things work together for good, for those who love the Lord and those who are called according to His purpose."* (NIV) My life was easier without the conflicts we suffered because of being unequally yoked. I have realized many other things over the years proving Romans 8:28 to be true, specifically related to that relationship.

I truly wish I had written down more specifically how the Lord has blessed me and provided for me over the years, yet I did not. Here are a few of the many ways in which I have been blessed. I am a registered nurse and was only working part time, so I could go right into full time employment at the hospital where I was already working. I received the house and car; he basically left with his clothes and tools. My standard of living did not change much. That was helpful. I had the support and love of friends in my church, and that was a huge blessing. I found a young lady from our church who would babysit for me. She lived close and was such a blessing to us. The girls loved her. I was given a promotion at work and received a raise, another huge blessing.

Divorce is an experience that does change your life forever. With God's help and support of friends and family one can survive and even thrive. I would never wish it on anyone and it is certainly not God's plan for any marriage, but the hard times in our lives prove to be the times of greatest growth. I learned more about prayer during that time and leaned on the Lord more than I had ever done. To quote the children's song, "My God is so big, so strong and so mighty, there's nothing my God cannot do!" I had gone to church all my life, but my God became so very real to me during that difficult time.

The Lord did bless me later with a wonderful man and we have been married 29 years. The girls were twelve and four years old when I remarried. I had been praying for eighteen months about finding a wonderful Christian man and I felt God provided him. We dated ten weeks and were married. I felt very comfortable and at peace with it because I had prayed about it for so long. I felt God had answered my prayers, even if he wasn't six feet tall, which had been one of the specific things I had asked for. He has been an incredible blessing to me.

One more side note about the miscarriages, I also recognized what a blessing child #2 was after losing four babies before her birth. I felt God knew what was ahead of me with the divorce and the challenges of single parenting, but he gave me another child, anyway. What an awesome God we serve!

Several years ago, I read the book "Heaven Is for Real". It the story of a four-year-old boy who experienced a life after death experience and went to Heaven. He saw a dark curly headed little girl in Heaven who he learned later was his sister his mother had miscarried before his birth. I knew my four babies had gone to be with the Lord, but their spiritual being had not yet really sunk in until I read that part in the book. I cried thinking I will literally get to see those precious little children I lost back so long ago. What a blessing that will be!

Have I been able to minister to others who have had miscarriages or had a divorce? Absolutely, many times over! 2 Corinthians 1:4 is true, *"who comforts us in all our affliction, so that we may be able to comfort those who are in any affliction, with the comfort with which we ourselves are comforted by God."* (NIV) God means so much to me and is so very real to me. I do not desire to go through those hard times again, but I know God will be with me and never forsake me, no matter what my future holds. What a truly awesome and amazing God we serve!

Chapter 10

Wounded Hearts

Growing up my family attended church not only three times a week, but were also involved in every other activity or event the church offered. Often, my parents were the ones who provided the organization and/or location for many of those activities or events that we were all able to enjoy for many years.

Our home life reflected a home where we prayed, worked, played, and shared together. The reputation of my parents' marriage and our family (parents, two brothers, and me) was above reproach. We were soybean farmers who had left the "safety net" of both of my parents' families in southeast Missouri to venture out on our own, just the five of us. We moved to the Mississippi delta where the church, neighbors, and friends became like family to us. My home life was not perfect, but it sure was more positive than negative, consistently.

"Things" began to change in my parent's 20-year old marriage that would lead to the end of our family as we knew it. As a teenager, we tend to view life from a different set of eyes than that of adults. When life seems grand and all in order and then what feels like "out of the blue", life can take a deadly turn, tear apart a family, and bring an onslaught of never before felt emotions.

My Mom

My mother was one of the most genteel, kindest, unassuming, and respected women I have ever known. She was often referred to as having a very "bubbly" personality. She taught many a Bible class at church, was always a teacher for vacation Bible school, drove tractors and bean trucks on the farm, made all my clothes in my younger years, and wow, could she cook! She also, ventured out into the community, joining "ladies clubs". She was the one who did not gossip, thus she knew a lot of personal information

77

about a lot of people. My mom loved to entertain in our home and could put together fine meals and decorations to meet any occasion revolving around fellowshipping with friends or family. She was a very happy and uplifting soul. I never knew anyone to say a negative thing about her. She knew how to be a friend and make friends.

My Dad

I was a daddy's girl, being the only daughter. He was 6'4 and had the biggest hands. He was a farmer. My dad could fix anything, had more common sense than several men put together, and was a bit of a dare devil. He was a man with a mission in life and was not afraid to take the risk farmers take in order to provide for the family and prepare for the next generation (my two brothers) to farm. Nurture and provide for our family is what my dad did. We had cars, trucks, boats, a swimming pool, an airplane, a lake house, and well just about anything a kid could want or need. I assure you money does not buy peace, love, and/or joy. Dad, too, was highly respected in the farming community. He also helped my mom prepare for house guest, church functions, or other activities that involved the use of our home for entertaining. My dad was active in church, teaching Bible class, being active in the worship service, and attending all men's business meetings to keep our small, but active church going. He was a good dad.

Their Marriage

My parents married right out of high school. Dad joined the Navy. Within about a year and a half my older brother was born, another year or so I came along, and then another year, or so my younger brother was born. We were a family of five by the time my parents were in their middle 20s.

When my brothers and I were ages one, two, and three, my parents moved us seven hours away from all of their families. We knew no one. My parents were very happily married. They depended on each other to make their farming venture a success. My parents enjoyed each other's company. During the winter months, they were forever playing Dominoes. Their marriage was peaceful, loving, and nurturing. Again, church was a central part of my parent's marriage and our family.

As the acreage of farm land increased, so did the money. As the money rolled in my parent's marriage began to waver. My dad was investing money, traveling, and enjoying trips to educate himself on the newest and best farm equipment. Mom traveled with my dad on most trips, but there were three teenagers at home. We were usually left behind to get ourselves to school. Farm kids can be pretty independent, resourceful, and reliable.

The Beginning of the End

I was in my first year of college and away from all the changes going on in my parents' relationship, the farming business, church involvement, and overall home life. My weekend visits home did not reveal a serious marriage problem was brewing until the spring of my freshman year in college. This is where my story picks up speed.

From March to August 21, 1981, my parents' marriage was all but over. Dad was having an affair. Both of my parents stopped going to church. My mom was devastated. She dearly loved my dad and had married him until death do them part. My dad became aloof, inattentive, and rather unconcerned about his entire family. My mom became horribly depressed, scared, and struggling to find any kind of peace. As the few short months progressed to August 21st, my mom's whole demeanor changed. She was not eating, sleeping, talking to anyone about the marriage problems, and saddest of all, she was trying her best to "win" back my dad's affection, but to no avail. I heard maybe four curse words leave my mother's mouth in my 18 ½ years with her, she never smoked or drank any kind of alcohol. Well, all that changed. I did not even recognize the woman she had become. She was a shell of a woman. My dad was not staying at the house that summer. I rarely saw him. It felt as though he was no longer part of our family.

The End Came Quickly

On August 21, 1981, I was in Tennessee with my mother's grandparents (my great-grandparents) when a late night call came from our preacher in MS. He told us that my mom had shot herself in the heart and had died that morning around 8:00. My dad discovered her body just a few hours before we got that phone call. As I pen my story, my heart is racing and my hands are shaky as I go back to hearing those words and how my world was turned upside down and inside out. That was 35 years ago. That kind of pain never, ever completely leaves ones memory or heart.

My dad was not helpful to my brothers and me as we were desperately grieving and missing our mom. By all accounts we lost both parents that day in August. It would be just over two years later that my dad lost the farm, our family house, and certainly, sense of financial security. Dad turned to his new "love" and moved in with her three months after mom died. He married her in December 1982. They had a son together the following year. Our relationship was shallow for the rest of his life. He died of cancer September 5, 2012.

The New Normal

For 13 years my new normal was packed full of life altering emotions, decisions, struggles, and destinations. It took me 13 years to find a place to put this horrible event in a place so that I could find peace to continue living and have a much brighter future. I wanted me back and I wanted a calm and peace back in my world, the kind I had growing up.

The first two years after my mother's death, I remember walking around like a very "spacey" person. This is what a state of intense shock can do to the mind. Some days it was a struggle to breathe. My heart physically ached and hurt. Nightmares were a constant dread. Bouts of wailing and crying would creep up on me and there was no gaining control. I had to just let it happen. Most of those hard tears crept up on me while I was in church services. My once superb attention to details became so disorganized in my thinking. I just could not concentrate. What I call "situational" depression set in and it took over all of my being. I did not have a bad case of the blues. I was in full blown depression.

A Christian who commits suicide is not oft put together words in the same sentence. Sadly, it does happen and sadly, suicide can happen to Christians. Two weeks after my mom died, I went to our home congregation for worship services. My mom's dead body lay in a casket in that building just two Sundays before that. One of our younger men preached that morning. We grew up with this guy. He knew our family very well. He was at the funeral. He stated that Christians who commit suicide don't have enough faith. (I am paraphrasing.) He did not mix his words, nor did he chew them well before he spit them out. We were all at a loss over my mother's death. What was he thinking? Obviously, those words stung and have stayed with me. I was able to allow God to do what he says, let Him be the judge of our actions and words. I did not allow the "where will my mom spend eternity" question torment or concern me. I knew then, and I know now, God is a good God and He will be just in His judgment of my mother's final act/decision in life. It was and is never my judgment call to make.

It was very hard to try to explain to anyone the whole situation leading up to my mom's death. People that knew her were grieving and at a loss themselves. It pained me to say the words "killed herself". I also knew that my mother's parents and siblings were pushing the detectives and police to take a closer look at my dad as the one who pulled the trigger. I had the police report. I knew the evidence was there that my mom pulled the trigger. I do believe my dad had his hand on her emotional trigger. The actions and response of my mother's family caused a lot of turmoil as I was trying to heal. Finally, the death certificate states cause of death was "suicide".

Where Was God

In 35 years, I never left God or the church. I have had my struggles growing in faith, but God was and continues to be a mightier source of power than anything I could ever do alone. God continually put people in my life that I needed to help me "keep the faith", function in life, make a living, and to encourage me. Having been raised on the Bible and being in the presence of many faithful Christians who were influential to me, I knew God did not "cause" this tragedy to transpire. I knew God was there to pick me up and carry me until I could stand alongside Him again. Never once did I blame God. God never, ever left my side! He continues to be right by me this very day. God was and is my primary source of strength regarding this tragedy and as life continues, God is my source of strength in good times and bad times.

What My Life Looks Like Today

I went back to college and got that degree in Social Work that I so wanted since I was in the ninth grade. While in my Social Work profession, a dear colleague who is a Licensed Professional Counselor (LPC) said it was time to take care of me and get my own depression in check. She said I needed counseling and our agency psychiatrist agreed. He put me on an anti-depressant! This is where life after 13 painful years takes a most positive turn. I was not happy with the LPC or Psychiatrist the first night on my medicine. That pill had me up almost all night with unbelievable energy. There was a simple fix to that, just change the time of day to take the pill. Wow! What a difference a day makes. The new medicine along with nine months of intense counseling, my world came back together. I could feel me returning with each passing day. One important detail that really made a huge difference was meeting my counseling goal of having a counseling session with my dad. I believe very strongly that God put that goal and ultimate session in place. It happened. I was able to ask my dad all those questions that had swirled in my mind for 13 years. I could ask him the questions that others planted in my mind about him. That was the best two hours and $160 I have ever spent on myself. The counselor facilitated the meeting and helped me ask those questions that I so desperately needed to have answered so I could move forward in my life. My dad knew it and he did what my "old" dad would have done, he obliged me. From that session forward, the nightmares ended, my concentration levels returned, and I found "me" again.

Today, I am a teacher for the visually impaired and blind in a county with several small schools. I travel to see my students at their respective school campus. I have never been more peaceful or happy in my life. The future is bright because God is front and center. He has prepared a home for me in heaven where there is no sin, sadness, sorrow, tears, or stress.

The Bible is my guide and I put a lot of faith, hope, and trust in those words inspired by God himself. One Bible character that resonates with me is Job. He suffered in a way I will never comprehend and yet, kept his unwavering faith in our God above. I understand "Be still and know I am God", Psalm 46: 10. Jesus tells us in Matthew 6: 25-34, "...not to worry about tomorrow..." and "...aren't the birds more important... Are you not more valuable than they?" Birds have become a constant symbol that God is right here with me every breath I take. I smile when I see any kind of bird. God is the key to surviving great losses, tragedies, the unexplainable, and the unexpected. If depression is an issue in your life or a loved one's life, God gave us a brain to get help. Depression is an illness that can take a life, just as diabetes, strokes, or heart attacks can kill.

Our Scars Of Hope

Chapter 11

Learning to Walk

As far back as I can remember I have always believed in God. I have always attended church. That being said, my belief today and the reason I attend church is different or at least understood.

We attended a Lutheran church growing up. We always dressed in our best. Hats and glove on Easter for us girls. Little suits and ties for the boys. Mom always took us. Dad didn't attend. I later found out that Dad had been married before, but his first wife didn't want children, so they divorced, and he was ex-communicated from the Catholic Church.

I do remember that I always believed that everything worked out for the best if I just let it happen. I didn't realize then that God could take what happened and give it purpose. His purpose. I continued through life and attending church because I believed that was what I was supposed to do.

I married when I was 25. It wasn't long before I knew that had been the wrong decision. But, because I believed in my vows, I wasn't going to leave the marriage. Then God helped me when I found out that he was having several affairs. In my mind, that was grounds for divorce, so I did.

It wasn't long before I would meet my current husband (of 30 years, so far) and we fell in love, got married, bought a house, and had a baby. What an exhausting first year!

At this time, I was still attending the Lutheran church. I faithfully took our son to Sunday school and church. At the time when my son should have started attending confirmation classes, I was working, and the timing didn't line up with getting him to classes. When I explained this to the preacher, he said that our son wouldn't get into heaven unless he was confirmed. This didn't set well with me. I quit going to that church.

After some time went by, I worked with a lady that I really admired. She was always calm, happy, everything I felt I wasn't. I can still remember thinking "I want what she has!" Eventually I attended church with her and I was hooked. I knew several people there and had been friends with some in high school. I got involved with the Worship team and our son got involved with the youth. We faithfully attended church and many events. I spent much time at church practicing with the Worship Team and doing what I could to help. I felt this was a true testament to my husband who didn't attend church and had questions about God.

Both my son and I had been sprinkled as infants. We were both baptized in this new church. Our son continued to grow in his faith, as well as me in my own faith, and understanding what a relationship with God was all about. Then the hard lessons came.

After years of confrontation with my husband about how much time I spent at church and not with him, I offered to step down from the Worship Team (which was my passion) thinking he would say not to. To my surprise, he said "Good". From that time on I learned to listen not only to what my husband said, but what his body language showed. That was the hardest thing I ever had to do.

I was attending a ladies bible study and the openness of all the ladies there, and my new best friend, who was my mentor on my Christian walk helped me grow. But sharing the struggles my husband and I had openly with my friends helped even more. They were able to give me scriptures and share their own experiences with prayer and what worked for their situations.

Since this time, my husband and I have grown closer. I have learned to depend on God first and that I don't have to attend every single event at church. He has even started asking questions. I do believe that he will become a believer, not because of me, but through me. I talk to him about my feelings and church stuff, not sugar coating it, because I don't want to give him a wrong impression of church life.

We recently retired after working abroad for several years. Those years were the best for us. I was able to concentrate on our relationship and he was willing to listen, learn what was important to me. I still have to respect him. That doesn't mean that I attend church every Sunday. If there is something that he needs help with, God knows where my heart is. It belongs to God first, and my husband second. The balancing act can be tricky at first, but with prayer it has worked. My husband has even commented on the changes I have made. Me making changes as shown me that when we do what God wants us to do, others change as well.

He is still not a confessed believer, but God and I are working on that. Balance has been reached for this time in our lives and through prayer I will continue to recognize change in both of us.

I should also mention that even through all of this, our son has attended and graduated from a local Christian College and received his degree in preaching. He is blessed. He has a gift of preaching and I know that God will use it to His advantage and glory. I have loved the time and knowledge our son has helped me gain. I will always cherish the long theological discussions we had sitting on the kitchen counters or going for a convertible car ride to our favorite ice cream place when we needed to talk.

I'll always be striving to follow where He leads me.

Chapter 12

Through Christ Who Strengthens Me

Betsy Arnold

"I can do all things through Christ who strengthens me."
Philippians 4:13

Caregiver. This word is both a title and an honor that I've carried for much of my life. Loss and grief. These are also words I've carried for much of my life.

Merriam-Webster defines the word caregiver as an individual who "gives help and protection to someone." With God's guidance, I've "given help and protection" to many people, in many ways throughout my life.

As a teenager, while most of my fellow junior high students were concerned about dating, friends, and student activities, I was taking care of both of my parents. To say I had to grow up quickly was an understatement. My mother had a second back surgery when I was 13, which caused her many recurring complications and pain throughout my teenage years. I became what my Dad referred to as "chief cook and bottle washer," not to mention nurse, physical therapist, and anything and everything to help my Mom heal. My father also had an illness at that time. He was in the public eye in local business and government. I helped to take care of him and protect his public image as best as a teenager could.

I was raised in church and believed in God. When I was 17 years old, I began a very personal relationship with Jesus Christ, which has grown tremendously throughout my life. He continues to be my strength every minute of every day.

Fast forward through the years to age 26, when I married a wonderful Christian man named Dale. We were looking forward to many long years of marriage, children, and all the adventures of living a normal life together. However, our life turned out to be anything but normal. Little did I know, my days of caregiving did not end with my teenage years. In fact, the caregiving I did as a teenager was merely training for what was to come. "I can do all things through Christ."

Before we were married, I knew that Dale was diagnosed at 13 years of age with a rare genetic blood disease called Cyclic Neutropenia. Two weeks into our marriage, my husband became very ill. Every 3 weeks the blood disease caused his white blood cell count to drop to very dangerously low levels. At those times, even a common cold could have killed him! He took steroids every three weeks to keep it at bay, because that is what his doctors at the time believed would be the most help. I spent many sleepless nights fighting high fevers and infections. During those nights, I would also cry and pray by his bedside. Even though he was in pain, my amazing husband continued to work full time, through illness and medication side effects. I worked several part-time jobs and went to school full time.

At the same time, in addition to taking care of Dale, my father began experiencing severe health issues. I helped my Mother to care for him and accompanied them to his doctor appointments. After many medical tests, my father was diagnosed with Stage 4 Acute Myeloid Leukemia. After two difficult rounds of strong chemotherapy failed to drive the cancer into remission, he was given a week to live. He was put on hospice at home. My family and I became his caregivers, which prolonged his life for 7 more weeks. We were grateful to have the extended time with him.

It was while my father was home on hospice that my husband began exhibiting very serious symptoms indicating a second blood disease. While helping to care for my father, I was also driving my husband back and forth to several doctors. Unfortunately, none of them had any answers. Dale's condition continued growing dire with each passing day. I confided in my Dad about what was going on. I told him everything I was doing to try and find answers, and that I was afraid it was blood cancer. My Dad sensed the urgency and concern in my voice and urged me to keep searching for answers, or it could be too late. He was right.

After my father's death, Dale continued to get sicker. With the help of my family, I got him to the right hospital. We found ourselves in the emergency room and subsequently admitted to a teaching hospital in St. Louis, Mo. Dale was diagnosed with a second blood disease called Henoch-Schonlein Purpura, which was caused by the Cyclic Neutropenia. We were then informed that he was the only one in the world with both blood diseases simultaneously! The doctors also told us that should we decide to have children, there was a 100% chance that he could pass down the first blood disease. Half of our children would get it and could die early. Dale saw himself lying in that hospital bed fighting for his life. Then and there, he made the decision not to have children. He didn't want to put his child through the suffering he had endured.

After my husband was diagnosed with the second blood disease, life changed drastically. We spent our lives going to many specialists, many times a week for an indefinite amount of time. My life as a caregiver changed drastically as well. With God's guidance, I now advocated for Dale at all his medical appointments. I spent many sleepless nights doing intensive research on both of his diseases and all his medications, which now included six months of chemo-therapy and high doses of steroids. I closely watched symptoms and patterns in both diseases and reported them to his trusted, world renowned medical team. His health improved and God blessed us with some semblance of a normal life for 6 years. We were grateful for that time and made many beautiful memories with family and friends.

Then the bottom dropped out. Dale was diagnosed with Myelodysplastic Syndrome (referred to by the head of the oncology department as a very lethal blood cancer) and ordered to have a stem cell transplant. I was not confident with the original oncologist assigned to my husband, so we flew across the country to Seattle, Washington to consult with the doctor who discovered the Cyclic Neutropenia. Since Dale was the only person in the world with both blood diseases, this doctor knew his case well. We also traveled to Ann Arbor, Michigan to consult with an oncologist who did stem cell transplants on patients with similar rare blood diseases. We were informed that Dale would make medical history by being the first patient with Cyclic Neutropenia to have a stem cell transplant. Because my husband wanted family and friends near, we came back to the hospital in St. Louis, closest to home, and found a different oncologist that we both felt confident in.

During this time, I began a blog on the Caring Bridge[1] website that kept everyone informed. This blog had many followers around the world, many that we had never met in person. People would log in every day to stay informed, and to send well wishes for us and pray for us. Having this kind of support made us feel less alone and was a tremendous blessing to us. It was also during this time that I was hospitalized after a trip to the emergency room, as doctors believed I was having a heart attack. It was discovered that my "heart attack" was in fact, an anxiety attack. After all that had transpired up to this point, it was no wonder. I was just glad that it wasn't Dale who was hospitalized that time.

Not long after, in the middle of a very stormy, rainy night, I drove to the store up the road for some medication for my husband, who was at home in bed. I was listening to our local Christian radio station. When I returned home and parked in our driveway, the rain started coming down in droves. The thunder pounded heavily, much like the storm going on in my own hurting, wounded heart. Why wasn't my husband getting better? After all the years I prayed for his healing, why wasn't it happening, and, moreover, why was his health getting much worse?

God knew what I was feeling. He knew the agony and the cry of my deepest heart. And He knew that since I was very young, music had always touched me very deeply. Right there in my driveway, with the storm raging outside, a song came on the radio called "Praise You In This Storm"[2] by Casting Crowns. These first lyrics of the song perfectly expressed what I was feeling:

---

[1] Caringbridge.org is a website which allows people to easily set up a caring message center to set-up updates and allow others to offer support and encouragement for a loved one during a crisis.

[2] "Praise You In This Storm" is a song recorded by contemporary Christian music band Casting Crowns, released by Beach Street and Reunion Records.

"I was sure by now, God, You would have reached down, and wiped our tears away, stepped in and saved the day. But once again, I say Amen, and it's still raining..." and at those words, I sat in my car and wept long and hard. Tears came pouring out of me as strongly as the rain pounded on the roof of my car. I felt like God was crying for me too, and saying "I'm with you." To this day, that song means more to me than I can ever express.

A severe infection in my husband's leg caused the transplant to keep being postponed. In the meantime, the cancer was advancing very rapidly and very aggressively. Because of this, the infection turned into Pyoderma Gangrenosum (Gangrene). Dale was hospitalized and once again was fighting for his life. Doctors were skeptical that he would survive the infection. Miraculously, his leg was healed, and he was finally healthy enough to schedule the transplant.

On the night before Dale's stem cell transplant, I found out I was pregnant. When I told him, we both cried. We believed that it would be a great incentive for his recovery, even knowing he could still pass down the first blood disease. We somehow knew that God would protect our child. But on the morning of the transplant, I had a miscarriage. We were grieving this loss as he was getting a new lease on life. Suddenly, life and death took on a whole new perspective.

After the stem cell transplant, my husband achieved remission! We were elated and grateful to God! During his initial recovery period, I found out I was pregnant again. But sadly, I miscarried the next day.

Soon after, Dale told me that his remission was only temporary. His body would reject the stem cells. Dale said that there would be a point when he would tell the doctors to stop treatment.
Indeed, my husband was prophetic. With all that transpired shortly after, I know now that God had spoken directly to him.

The stem cells began rejecting just two weeks shy of reaching a milestone that would signify complete and total remission. The

---

Written by Mark Hall and Bernie Herms and produced by Mark A. Miller, it was released on January 28, 2006 as the second radio single from the band's 2005 album Lifesong.

doctors began treatment for stem cell rejection, and warned us that if the rejection went to his lungs, it would be very hard to fight. After 11 months of fighting rejection in other areas of the body, it did in fact, reach his lungs. He was hospitalized for the last time. I practically lived in his hospital room. The hospital was gracious enough to bring in another bed so that I could stay by his side.

Philippians 4:13 became our signature scripture. It became "We" can do all things through Christ who strengthens "us" to include both my husband and myself. With every torturous procedure and test that was done to try and save his life, I repeated that scripture. I wrote it in my blog entries, which by then, had reached thousands of readers. Dale and I became a strong force together, both sharing our strong faith in Christ through the blog, and with all who would step into that hospital room. In our weakness, during our toughest battle, Christ was our strength.

Because the stem cell rejection was now everywhere, my husband stopped eating. The treatments that the doctors were doing were not working. Dale made the decision to stop all treatments. After a month in the hospital, he came home on hospice care, which I provided. After exactly a week on hospice, my husband died, in a hospital bed in our living room on Halloween, at the age of 43. Being his caregiver was my life for our 18+ years of marriage. He was the love of my life.

In addition to my being a caregiver since I was a teenager, I have also been a musician since I was 5 years old. I was in my second year of college, studying and training to be a music therapist when Dale died. The logical combination of caregiving and music became music therapy. Dale strongly believed that this was the career God had for me. It was my original intent to have a career and to be able to financially support him after his transplant, but God had other plans. In fact, my caregiving duties resumed after I finished my degree. I became a full-time caregiver to my Mother, who had COPD. For the next two years, I gave my life, day and night to take care of her in any, and every way I could until her unexpected death from suspected liver cancer, diagnosed only a week before. This was a huge shock and rocked my world to the core. My Mom and I took care of each other, just as my husband and I had taken care of each other. The only full-time jobs I ever knew were taking care of the two of them.

After my Mom's death, anxiety, depression, and loneliness controlled my life. I developed a chronic illness which almost took my life not long after. My parents and my husband were my best friends. We all loved each other completely unconditionally and took care of each other. Now they were gone, and I was left to take care of myself. I always felt that their lives were much more important than mine, and that taking care of them was my entire life.

I took the Certification Board for Music Therapists several times and didn't pass it. Without board certification, prospective employers would not hire me. I thought that my purpose was to be a Board Certified Music Therapist. I thought that would be my career, my way to financially support myself. Since I couldn't pass the Board, I wondered what I could do. I worried obsessively about losing my home. It was a big part of my heart, because this house is where my husband and I lived, and where he breathed his last. My house is located across the street from the house that I grew up in. It has always been home to me, no matter wherever else I lived. The threat of losing it loomed large. After everything I've done to always help and to take care of others, why was all this loss happening to me? The anxiety, depression, and loneliness consumed me, and I wondered; who takes care of the caregiver?

I felt very alone in learning how to take care of myself and financially supporting myself. I didn't know how I was going to survive, or, if I even wanted to. That's how deeply messed up I was after experiencing all those very significant losses. I reached out to others, but no one was stepping up to give me the answers I so desperately needed.

But God has stepped up. He has had a purpose all along for my life. He has shown me that He is my Caregiver. He is taking care of my every need, and He has all along. He has been preparing me for such a time as this. I am working many hours a week for a home care company as a caregiver. It's something I thought I would never do again, but I absolutely love it! Not only do I get to carry on my legacy of caregiving, I get to do music therapy! And God is saving my home! I also have several part-time jobs playing the piano for several places, touching the lives of others with the music He has given me to share. I am truly blessed.

Because of Him, I am doing so many things I never thought I could ever do. I'm earning a living doing what I absolutely love, and there are more jobs on the horizon. I get to help people almost every day! God has also brought others in my life in the form of trusted friends who love me and help me. I get to love and help them too! Life does go on after loss. I truly can do "all things through Christ who strengthens me."

God has shown me through all the years of unfathomable loss and grief that He will "never leave me nor forsake me." (Hebrews 13:5). God is the ultimate Caregiver. He knows who I am. He understands me. He has given me beauty for ashes in the aftermath of incredible loss. He has given me purpose. He has given me hope. He has given me everything. He is my strength. And He can be your strength, too.

*A few of Betsy's song lyrics are shared on the next few pages.

I Will Take Your Hand

Lyrics and music© by Betsy Arnold

Through the longest night, I'll be there for you.
I will take your hand and gently lead you through.
Through the darkest valley, you won't be alone.
I will take your hand and safely guide you home.

When the rain falls down and the cold winds blow
When you can't find your way and don't know where to go
When the gray skies beckon and the sun won't shine
I will take your hand; put your hand in mine.

When it feels like your world is crashing down
And you don't know what to do
And you're praying for life to turn around
I will take your hand, and I'll take care of you.
In your darkest hours, when no one else is there
I will take your hand, and be with you in prayer
We'll pray that God will heal you, and when our journey's through
I will take your hand and live my life with you.

We'll pray that God will heal you, and when our journey's through
I will take your hand and live my life with you.

Live Strong

Lyrics and music© by Betsy Arnold

When you're up against a wall
And you feel your hope is small
And life keeps getting harder every day
When you hurt deep inside your soul
Remember God is in control
And He will work it out in His own way

Live strong
When the road ahead is long
And you feel life go all wrong, keep movin' on
Live strong
Hold your head up proud and high
Life is worth another try
God knows the reason why
Live strong

When the pain has got you down
And there is bad news all around
And the faith that you once had is all but gone
Turn to God to see you through
And He will take care of you
He will show you what to do
Live Strong
Live strong
When the road ahead is long
And you feel life go all wrong, keep movin' on
Live strong

Hold your head up proud and high
Life is worth another try
God knows the reason why
Live strong

Even when the road ahead seems so long
You can go the distance if you live strong

Live strong
When the road ahead is long
And you feel life go all wrong, keep movin' on
Live strong
Hold your head up proud and high
Life is worth another try
God knows the reason why
Live strong

Stay By My Side
Lyrics and music© by Betsy Arnold

Walking down this long, hard road
I am worn and weary.
Please take my hand, and lead me home.
Lord, I need you near me.

Stay by my side.
God, be my guide.
Lead me through the valley
To the other side.
Please make me whole
Deep in my soul.
I'll be okay if You'll stay.
Stay by my side.

And now I see the life You have for me
And how You've prepared me.
Please guide my way each and every day.
Lord, I need You there with me.

Stay by my side.
God, be my guide.
Lead me through the valley
To the other side.
Please make me whole
Deep in my soul.
I'll be okay if You'll stay.
Stay by my side.

Chapter 13

"PURE GRACE"

By Caetlin Ann

I have attempted writing my story several times and once I was nearing its end, I lost it by a compromised computer. I couldn't believe all my work had vanished. I wondered how God could allow something so sensitive and labor intensive be lost. I was upset that God didn't protect my story. I recalled how I wrestled with this same issue in year's past- why didn't God protect my story? Why didn't He protect ME? I had to start fresh. That's one of the beauties of God's nature. He allows us to start over-a new chapter, a new life.

Over the thirty plus years of walking with the Lord, I have learned that there are running themes in everyone's life, whether they be blessings, success, addictions or poor health. My story isn't any different. I remember thinking at an early age that I was special to God, but it seemed the enemy was going to do whatever he could to take me down. Satan is a liar and his wiles and ways are not creative at all. He tried to take me down weaving themes through my life.

I was raised in a large, Midwestern, Catholic family-the first five of us were step ladder in grade and age. Being the middle of seven made it easy to get lost in the shuffle or forgotten by whatever drama presented itself. I also had many first cousins, most of us being the same age or in the same grade, many of us attended the same church and schools. Getting lost wasn't difficult at all, but that's not what I wanted. I wanted the same as any little girl-to be delighted in; what every woman desires-to show her beauty.

The themes of my story began at an age too vulnerable to protect myself, in a vague memory that remains securely locked in

101

a closet, even after all these years. But it is a place where the enemy began his attempts of destruction for what God had planned for me from the beginning. *"My frame was not hidden from you when I was made in the secret place. When I was woven together in the depths of the earth your eyes saw my unformed body. All the days ordained for me were written in your book before one of them came to be." (Psalm 139:15-16 NIV)* This memory, with my sister fifteen months my junior, remains blurred, but the hauntings of my mind suggest we were taken into a dark room and sexually violated. Even though our ages were too tender to recall the details of this account, it resulted in years of bedwetting for both of us. Neither my parents nor we could account for this problem other than "laziness" or "carelessness;" we were shamed and humiliated. It wasn't until years later when psychology took a place in the world for those with such problems, and not just the ones with serious mental disorders, that an understanding for the patterns of my behaviors began to unfold. Until then I had to endure the ridicule and shame. The humiliation of this followed me to elementary school as it was shared by one neighborhood friend to a classmate. **Shame**! One of those running themes in my life.

The years leading into my adolescence were met with intermittent violations by close family members; I couldn't escape it. Now I wanted to be lost, unseen, and yet there was a place inside where I was receiving the attentions I so longed for. This was very confusing for a young girl-this kind of touch felt good. No one had to tell me, but I knew it was wrong. I didn't look for it, nor did I desire it. But why did it seem that wherever I turned a man or boy would seek these attentions from me? I needed to escape this. I needed to hide. Another theme-**get lost, hide yourself.**

In my biblical studies I learned that sin follows a family, *("...for I the Lord your God, am a jealous God, punishing the children for the sins of the fathers to the third and fourth generation of those who hate me..." Exodus 20:5 NIV)*. When I began to reason with these truths on my road to healing, I wanted to understand why these sins also followed me from outside of my family. Was I a magnet for abuse? I remembered wondering if all men would misuse me. My young adult years would speak a resounding "yes" to this question. This theme - **sexual perversion**.

It wasn't until my early teens when I became assertive enough to protect myself that this abuse stopped. I grew into a very awkward and insecure 'me.' What child doesn't experience that? But my secrets seemed to have magnified this reality. I couldn't let anyone in. More shame; more hiding.

My adolescent and early teen years were amid the "Energy Crisis." The oil was low, and unemployment was high. My family was not estranged to the effects of this. Just when I thought life would become 'normal', something would follow which continued an infringement on my peace. My father's unemployment lasted over a year and his drinking began to increase. Perhaps the world's crisis had something do with this. Perhaps his family's sin line had its own effects on this behavior. His father and brother were alcoholics. Another theme-**addiction.** By the time I was in high school, his drinking became more frequent and many of my nights were plagued with yelling and dish throwing until the wee hours. This made early class schedules difficult.

Despite all this, I remained somewhat naïve about life. My older siblings found comfort in recreational drugs, until my oldest brother found Jesus, or, as I would later learn, Jesus rescued him. Each one of us would find that life transformation down the road, but until we were on the same trajectory, I contended with life and school as a very average student, hiding. Riding with my popular, older sister and her very cool friends did not make high school any easier. Their "recreational drug" use in the car, most every morning, made my average grades become less than average. I started to fit in less with any social group, which is very important in high school. I was involved in music, so I wasn't really accepted by the kids who partied. I started smoking my sophomore year and had family members known for recklessness, so I wasn't in with the straight kids either. My academics didn't qualify me for the nerds and my lack of athletic ability meant I didn't hang with the jocks. It was easy to hide.

The summer before my junior year, my mother finally left my father and moved me and my three younger siblings out of our childhood home. Some of my neighborhood friends had gotten pregnant or dropped out of school anyway; all but one. She was bright and studious, unlike me. I was in survival mode, but at least now the effects of my father's drinking were gone, and I wouldn't be high by the time I got to school every morning.

However, that year would prove not to be as peaceful as I had hoped. Shortly after school began, I learned that my cousin, who was a close friend and whose age separated us only by one month, was reported missing. She had a history as a runaway, so the police were not quick to start a search. For months I was grilled by my mother to see if I had any idea of her whereabouts. Truth be told, we started to drift apart just before summer ended that year. Regardless, her absence haunted me. It remained until the following spring when I returned from school one evening after hours of practice for the school musical. My arms filled with costumes and a song in my heart for my mother's birthday, I was met with her running out the door and my sister telling me the news of my cousin's body being found. "BODY?" ... "FOUND?" I dropped everything in my hands. I could sense the bile in my stomach churning. I couldn't have heard the words correctly. My knees gave way and I found myself on the floor atop my costumes. She was raped and killed; her body left in a field almost 5 months until the snow melted...identifiable only by her dental records. The funeral procession was one unlike anything seen in our small town. The motorcade lasted almost a mile. The effects of her death lasted longer.

I managed to make it through the rest of high school unscathed, but I had neither the money nor grades for scholarships to attend college. Honestly, it wasn't even on my radar, but I had no idea what I was going to do with my life. I had grand aspirations of travel and adventure, but neither the means or knowhow to accomplish them. It seems I wasn't the only one who knew this. A boyfriend of sort wrote this about me in one of his senior books. "Knows what she wants but doesn't know how to get it." Maybe I wasn't very good at hiding after all.

The military was quick to come to my rescue; or so I thought. My trip into the big city of Chicago to swear my life for country was accompanied by recruiters providing alcohol to under-aged and vulnerable girls. Whereas I had never volunteered myself to anyone before, these men took advantage of the situation and I found myself acquiescing to the pressures of my assailant. Since my perception of authority was distorted and wrecked with fear, it would not be the last time this would happen. I would later learn how to use sex to my advantage.

Before Uncle Sam sent me on my longed-for adventures, I had a brief interlude with God. It was an isolated and unique experience. The encounter fed into my childhood thoughts about me and God. As I lay in bed one evening, I began to pray with a rosary in hand, something I had done from the time I was a young girl. I knew there was something about prayer which drew me in, even though I didn't really understand the power behind it. I got through the myriad of "Hail Mary's" and began to pray, what is commonly known as "The Lord's Prayer." Something was happening. I could feel myself leaving my body, or could I? There was another presence in my room and I knew it. I had been inundated enough with my brother's evangelism to believe this was something bigger than me. I began to weep uncontrollably. These were not tears of remorse or repentance, rather tears of the incredible love and acceptance I felt. Surely this was the "born again" experience my brother frequently spoke of. After some time, my tears changed in anguish for my friends and family who still didn't know God. I wanted everyone to experience this. The presence finally left. Now what?

After this, I was soon assigned overseas, where the undercurrents of all my pain started to manifest. The adventures I had longed for also provided me unrestricted alcohol consumption, which I willingly used to help cover up this pain. As these poor life choices increased, my inhibitions decreased resulting in a life of greater promiscuity. I needed more alcohol-more interludes-more shame-more pain-more alcohol.

Even though my life seemed to spiral downward, the impressions of my Catholic upbringing forced me to continue attending mass. Since I had that brief encounter, I continued to feel a constant pull on my wayward heart. The contradiction of this accepting God wrestled with my distorted understanding of a punitive God. Despite my earlier experience, I still found it hard to believe he could actually love me with everything I had done.

Somehow, I was able to hide my behavior to a select few. Those who saw me at church ONLY saw me at church and thought I was special to God. (How could people see things in me when I was just trying to hide?) But those who really knew me, knew a darker side. All my themes seem to have collided-**shame-sexual perversion-addiction-HIDE!**

By the early 80s I was stateside again, living in Texas. I felt like I could finally make a clean start. But there was still a gravitational pull towards my old life and I quickly reconnected with an old friend from Spain who had been reassigned in California. I took a military commuter plane to see what kind of escapades we could experience. She and I, along with one of her roommates, agreed to take advantage of my brother's convenient residence in Los Angeles and went to visit for Easter weekend. They were days filled with sightseeing and becoming reacquainted with his family. Since my brother was no longer practicing Catholicism, we attended an Assemblies of God church on Easter. I have no recollection what was preached, but something began to happen. I felt my heart beating out of my chest and was sure everyone could hear it. What was happening to me? I was crying, and I didn't know why. Was this the same God I encountered before? I let it go. No one asked me anything, so maybe they didn't see it. Or did they? I was able to quickly put whatever it was aside to make our way down to Mexico for more tourism; but whatever was happening to me wouldn't end there.

As my friends made their way back home, I decided to stay on a few extra days. A friend of my brothers had gotten my attention. It could have been our mock wedding at Knott's Berry Farm, or just his gregarious personality and humor that drew me in, but I wanted to see what would come of it. That week, I was inundated with Jesus, from this man who would later become my husband, my brother and sister in law-two Bible studies in one week. Who does that? There was no escaping this move in my life. After my brother finished sharing the gospel, he offered an invitation to me. "XXXXX, are you ready to ask Jesus into your heart?" What? What does that even mean? But then something happened. I had another encounter with this God, which has only happened one other time in my life. I heard an audible voice. It said, "XXXXX, I

106

love you, and you don't have to go to bed with me to receive this love." This was very personal and very profound. My God did love me. He loved ME! And so on April 7, 1983, I finally made a decision to let something greater than me lead my life. At that moment, my feet hit the ground and I haven't looked back. But that was salvation...I needed healing...lots of it.

Several years into my walk with God, I began to have very elicit dreams which haunted me. It made it difficult for me to live out who God had called me. The meanings of my names are 'pure' and 'grace'. Grace seemed easy at the time, but purity was difficult when I had all this shame following me. I heard the enemy remind me of those themes. "If they only knew who you really are...what you've done." Quick-**HIDE!** If it were just these voices, perhaps I could have managed this façade I maintained with my new church friends. But I had begun a real relationship with my mock husband, who unbeknownst to me, had secrets of his own. But this man wasn't like the other men-he was a believer in Christ like me; surely, he would not lead me down a path of destruction. But the broken places in my heart and limited understanding of Christianity made it difficult to understand boundaries and his secrets didn't respect boundaries. God would not let me go. I began my road of personal healing.

The secrets he had were not discussed openly. In the world of psychology sexual addictions were reserved for perverts, pedophiles and rapists. It definitely wasn't used to describe *normal* people. But this ugly theme of **sexual perversion** crept into my life once again. It wasn't until years into our relationship and later our marriage that this addiction was given a name. Now I was living with this man and the boundaries became even more skewed. I had secrets of my own and trying to hide his made life worse. We were in Bible College, preparing for the ministry. We'd better **hide!** Eventually, we couldn't hide any longer. I finally sought counseling, and this continued for years at different places, with different people. When my husband would not participate, I continued seeking ways to let God heal my past. However, the tentacles of my husband's addiction to pornography made physical intimacy difficult and it fed into the shame I associated with sex. It

107

also destroyed many ministry opportunities, our finances, and eventually, our marriage.

After years of counseling, I found the collision of my themes repeating itself. These "sins of the father" were now affecting my family. I had taken my sins to the cross whenever the Lord brought a memory to the forefront of my mind. I forgave and broke off familiar spirits and generational curses. I claimed scriptures which spoke of the new creation within me. I grabbed hold of whatever I could to preserve what was left of my family. But something still haunted and lingered in our home.

The effects of pornography are staggering. In an attempt to provide statistics for this chapter, I found myself swimming in information which brought tears to my eyes and made my heart sick. Its epidemic effect is so wide spread that you would almost never know who is using. He looks like your brother or your boss. She looks like your girlfriend involved in "erotica" or your best friend who goes from one relationship to another. It takes on the form of human trafficking of young boys and girls. It results in the destruction and breakdown of the family unit. It looked like my family; it looked like me.

Learning of possible violations against my own daughters made my heart ache in such a way that made it difficult to breathe. Seeing my life repeated in the hearts of two beautiful girls forced me to reach out for something greater than me. I could only return to that presence, that voice that LOVE that was greater than me. God made himself more real to me than anything I had experienced in the past. It was not an easy road. It was wrought with pressing in and laying hold of promises when I wanted to bail time and time again. It sent me on short drives where I pounded the steering wheel as I yelled and scream at God. It was filled with divine revelations of His faithfulness, His love for me, His purpose and preservation of my life. Finally, I felt clean. I felt pure. I was pure.

Many years had passed since God began the restoration of my life, but I still had one more bout with the enemy's themes. I did what I knew to do to be healed, forgiven, and whole. I participated in "Divorce Recovery" (a Biblical program to assist those affected by divorce.) I remained accountable to leadership and the disciplines of personal spiritual growth. I began to lead small group discussions for women. I disciple them, provided one-on-one mentoring and healing. I counselled women to put on two pair of running shoes and 'high tail it' out of questionable relationships. I pursued God. I had others begin to praise my wisdom and growth. I think I heard it enough that I believed it myself. Little did I know that I was being set up to do a deeper work for God.

Pride can be very subtle. Often, we think of arrogance or conceit, but pride takes on many forms; like judgment. My counsel to women would often be seeded in judgment, covered with my sage advice to rectify their poor life choices. And then I fell. I fell hard. *(Pride goes before destruction, a haughty spirit before a fall. Proverbs 16:18 NIV)*

I had been separated and divorced seven years when I became involved with a married man. When I gave my heart over, I didn't know he was married. But even upon learning this information, trying to break free from the relationship was difficult. I had not dated since my husband, let alone be physically involved with anyone. I was now the one making poor life choices and I didn't want to stop. It was obvious to everyone, including me, that this man had no regard or respect for me, but his pursuit was hard and fast, and I was addicted to his presence. I behaved like someone who did not know God. I lied to those who loved me. I turned my back on what I believed. But God, in his loving mercy, surrounded me with godly men and women, and a sister who prayed. They didn't judge my actions or even try to change them; they were eager to help me get to the root of the problem.

It was during this time when God began to speak to me in words that I cannot explain. Deeper healing from those tentacles were stripped away. I experienced healing and restoration of my body, soul and spirit. I began to have a vision again for what He called me into twenty-five years earlier. I experienced such an incredible measure of grace that I began to see the heart of the Father on another level; I had become grace.

It is easy to slip back into what we know or understand. I knew how to hide, how to let shame identify me. I understood addiction and sexual perversion. The enemy of my soul was nearby and

109

quick to remind me of my past. But over the years, I learned the character of God. His voice became louder and eventually drowned out the other. I learned that His very image is born out in my hosting His presence. I had to learn how to trust that; I still do.

In pursuit of my God, He proved himself faithful to take me into places that cannot be defined by words. When I tapped into the natural ways of God, I saw supernatural manifestations in the reality of who God says I am. I am His image bearer. I am loved intrinsically. I am "pure". I am "grace." I am PURE GRACE.

Final Proof

I am not worthy of your love, or to even speak your name.

And every time I try to pray, I get crippled by my shame.

I hear the voices loud and clear, "you'll never be good enough".

But I call the devil out by name,

So, he knows I've called his bluff.

The lies he tells me every day can't be further from the truth.

Because Jesus died and rose again,

His love for me the PROOF.

By Taylor Miller

Chapter 14

"Telltale Text"

The text flashed across my screen while my son and I were texting one Friday night. "I am done with work let's go get high".

Now, no one asks his mother to go get high with him. Clearly this wasn't meant for me, but God meant for me to receive it. I knew it wasn't a joke. We had been concerned something was wrong for quite some time, but all our attempts to discuss were met with denial. This was the truth text we were needing-a tool to confront with a little more evidence.

God answers prayers in very creative ways and, as painful as this was, I recognized God was giving us an opening to get to the bottom of a very long journey. And, so the story begins.

"Though the fig tree should not bloom, and there be no fruit on the vine, though the yield of the olive should fail, And the fields produce no food, Though the flock should be cut off from the fold, and there be no cattle in the stalls, yet, I will exult in the Lord, I will rejoice in the God of my salvation. He is my strength and He will make my feet like hinds' feet. And, makes me walk on my high places."
Habakkuk 3:17-19 NAS

I first found this verse in 1982. It was one of those that jumped off the page at me. Maybe it's because we are farm/ranch people, and we live in the mountains, and like to hike. Maybe it's because God knew I would need to return to it over and over in my journey of life. For whatever reason, it became my "verse." In the margins of my bible are variations of that verse that mark upsetting events-grappling moments when I was frustrated, scared, or hopeless.

"...though the kids are coughing and wheezing and there have been several hospitalizations, a diagnosis of asthma and lots of sick days, though I am bone weary, yet, I will rejoice in the God of my salvation, the Lord God is my strength, we will get through this, we will walk healthy again- Habakkuk 3:17-19 (Author's paraphrase)

"...though the debt is mounting and there have been some rough financial years, and there is no easy way around all this, Yet, I believe God will walk us over this mountain, I will exult in the Lord,...I will rejoice. Habakkuk 3:17-19 (Author's paraphrase)

Sometimes I didn't feel like rejoicing but I made myself look to God, my Father and look around at all I had to be thankful for. Some days my prayer was, "I can't rejoice today Father, I will try again tomorrow. Please help me."

All I ever wanted to be was a wife and a mom and I was blessed four times over. I wanted a Christian family and found my soul mate who agreed; this would be our path. We survived the turmoil of the 70s and started our married years seeking God. We were Christians, but I knew there was more than just going to church. I was given a book, The Christian Family by Larry Christenson even before we were parents and I said, this is what I have been looking for: Biblical principles, Biblical truth. I thought I had the formula-our family would be perfect. No child of mine would get lost to drugs as we had seen friends do in the 70s.

So, I was immature and idealistic, but aren't we all at times? I had to accept there was no magic formula and no easy answers in life on this earth. The good news was, I knew God was in control and working overtime in all the challenges. I knew His ways were not my ways and I could trust. The challenges mentioned above, sick children, financial stress, lost dreams, these were God's way of getting my attention, of letting me know *Who* was in control of growing my faith and family. The Word of God became truth and light to strengthen and comfort me.

Infants grew into toddlers, toddlers to school-age kids, middle schoolers to high schoolers. There were backpacking trips, picnics, sporting and school events, playing down at the creek, family
bicycle rides to Mrs. Olson's for breakfast, baptisms, graduations, and birthday celebrations! It was a busy blur, but we enjoyed our

busy life and teenagers – we really did. Looking back, I can't pinpoint where I lost him, but somewhere along the line I did.

My mom always said when your kids are little they step on your toes and when they are grown they step on your heart. My heart was ripped right wide open that Friday night the text came through. So, what do you do with one broken heart? You hand the pieces to a loving God. Our faith is developed for times like these, even though I wished for anything, any other challenge but this.

This kid loved basketball; he slowly gave up all other sports to focus on this one. He had a goal of going to and maybe even winning state. That never happened. Then he discovered he was too small to play in college, even in the small college he attended. He played intramurals and "hung" with the athletes. When he called the spring of his sophomore year sobbing, I heard the words "my best friend took his own life last night, mom. We spent yesterday together hanging out; I didn't see it coming. He was captain of the football team – everything I wanted to be." The pain was oozing from his broken heart.

I feel this was the beginning of a downward spiral even though he said he was seeing a counselor to help with the grief. This was so huge. Why this child God? I prayed. He was my most sensitive child, the quiet observer, the encourager of others. He had a great sense of humor and could break the family tension with a funny quip or comment. Looking back, I now see these special traits began to seep away over time, starting this sophomore year in college.

A DUI the summer of 2006, a month after he returned from college, without a signed diploma, was a red flag, but again in my naivety he always talked me down and away from the issue.

He was floundering and we could see it, but he would not let us approach the real issues. We watched the bank account. Money wasn't disappearing without a reasonable explanation; he could get up and do physical work beside his dad after late nights. I kept talking myself out of the thought he was possibly in trouble with drugs or alcohol. "Weren't we a little crazy in our growing-up years?" my husband would always point out. We had no family history of substance abuse that I knew of then.

The DUI was devastating to me, but his attitude was the most disturbing. "Oh, Mom, everyone gets a DUI these days, it's no big deal." Mr. Tough Guy soon learned it was a big deal. Two years of working through the system, counseling, and probation followed. He spent his 25th birthday in jail and then was sentenced to one year of work release. He opted for this over losing his license for a year and we agreed natural consequences were necessary. I had to swallow my pride and just trust.

As the summer of 2008 started, our son decided he would transfer his credits to a state university closer to home and finish out his student teaching. Within a few weeks, he had a place to live, a job in the city and transcripts on their way. A new leaf was turning, and it all seemed positive. He just needed to student teach and then he would have a college degree and a purpose in life, but a semester turned into another two years. Goodness, what is taking so long. He was always a little vague with "they didn't accept all my credits", which was true. "I decided to add secondary education to my classes to increase my chances of a job." It was his life, we needed to let him find his way.

Still, something seemed drastically wrong. He continued to withdraw and be absent even when he was right there in the room. There were no arguments, slammed doors, or ugly scenes, but a constant worry in my heart that he was on drugs. Any attempts to have a serious conversation were diverted or diluted. He agreed to counseling, and we had sessions together, and sessions alone. In the end the counselor summed up our time with "Everything is fine, he just doesn't want to grow up." Really?? I remember thinking: this was a waste of time. And that's when my fervent prayers turned desperate. God please help us reach him and discover how to help him.

A few weeks later the infamous text flashed on my phone.

My husband and I took a few weeks to gather advice, recruit prayers and read. How do we confront our son without pushing him farther away, was the question of the hour? I had kept the text, planned a nice dinner and invited him to come. Over dessert I pulled up the text and quietly asked if he was on drugs and if he needed help. He was stunned and a bit speechless for a few seconds, then denied it, and said it was a joke and gave us the famous words,

"Everything's fine." He didn't want to linger. "Truth will set you free, we will always love you no matter what," I cried as he walked to the door, shoulders sagging. He quietly left, and I fell to my knees. God, this is not going in the right direction.

The next day my husband received a barrage of phone calls from our son's friends, "How could we accuse him of doing drugs? He was so above that and would never do drugs." Then the truth came. "He drinks too much, but he would never do drugs."

My husband went to our son, who now was quite angry that we would accuse him of using drugs. Really? Couldn't he see alcohol was a drug, and we were trying to help him? In his wisdom, my husband stayed calm and just said, "We don't know what you are doing, but something is wrong. You have pulled away from the family and all the things you used to love. You were our star basketball player, you loved the game, you wanted the ball, you wanted to make plays and win, you worked hard, and you were a leader. Mom and I don't know what it is, but it's clear you don't want the ball any more. You don't want in the game."

That's when our son broke, the sobs came, and he said, "It's alcohol, dad. I drink too much and I can't control it anymore." The alcohol that had once been fun had its ugly clutches on him and he was addicted. Hard alcohol was his drug of choice. Binge drinking through college had sped the process up and he was addicted big time.

An overwhelming sadness consumed me for many months. I choked on the words "our son is an alcoholic", even though I knew the truth was a necessary step in the healing process. If there had been a hospital for hope, I would have checked myself in. I had to work through the emotions of anger, fear and despair. I had to find my faith viable, and I had to hope, or I was no use to anyone. And in all this my heart was breaking for him, for all his anxiety, hurts and shame.

I had always told the kids "it's not wrong to have problems, it's wrong to deny them." Problems need to be worked on and our faith is a tool to help. Even in all our pain, I knew God was in this. He has to be or there would never be any hope.

It took a few months but our son finally desired help and agreed to and found a residential treatment center. After 30 days he was out with a new outlook. I thought we had our work and plan and could move forward with the worst behind us. God had other plans.

Two years he was sober, working his program, working a good job, seemingly leaving the old ways behind. They told me relapses were normal and a part of the journey. It still hit me hard when once again we sat down and discovered the alcohol had crept back into his routine. This one scarred heart tore open again and God reminded me He was my strength and song.

It's been a long six years. I have learned a lot about the disease, my faith, my son. There have been 4 residential treatment stays from 30 to 90 days. Detox, counseling, classes, out-patient therapy, A-A, and Al Anon. Relapses, over and over. Health issues. Ruined holidays, happy holidays, good moments and bad moments. Two steps forward, one step back.

God is right there every moment weeping with me, reminding me of His promises, giving me hope. He didn't promise me it would be easy.

It is a disease of relationships they said in counseling and those word were bitter in my mouth I had worked on what I thought was a strong family, a loving Christian family. Did I fail? No.

You know what, we are a strong Christian family, using our faith to confront an addiction and help others. We never were perfect and we never will be. Would I do some things differently? Maybe. Hind sight is always wiser, but in all this, God has become real to me in a way He never had been before. We, as a family have had to figure out how to live in the face of unspoken pain. We had to find a new normal, we had to love and love and forgive and forgive and it has made us more real, more compassionate and less judgmental. This was the journey we were given. Your journey can make you better or it can make you bitter I once heard. We are choosing better.

This week the principle verse that comforted me was, "In the Hands of God, intended evil becomes eventual good." It's based on Romans 8:28. I believe this. My job is to continue to love, support and give our son hope. I'm to wait on God's timing and believe addiction can be resolved and end in recovery. It's up to our son every moment of every day. It's an ugly disease.

Scars of hope are in all of us. I had always thought a scar was a healed wound-a mark reminding you of some painful moment, but Webster defines a scar as a wound or sore that has not completely healed.

That's where we are today. Not completely healed. Still in process, still fitting pieces back together. Taking one day at a time. Still hoping.

I look for hope everywhere, every day, and it's there. A friend hands me a small box of chocolates with the word 'Hope' across the top. Another person says in a meeting, "as long as we are breathing, there is always hope!" My son texts, "today is a good day mom." A devotion states that there are 166 verses in God's word about hope. Biblical hope is not just a hope, but a knowing.

"Though there is an addiction in our family and many relapses, though the journey is long and painful at times, though the statistics are not on our side, I will ask for a miracle. I will rejoice. I will hope and know the Lord God is my strength. He will bring us safely over this mountain of disease." Habakkuk 3:17-19 (Author's paraphrase.)

Today I read, "For the vision is yet for the appointed time, it hastens toward the goal, and it will not fail, though it tarries, wait for it; for it will certainly come..." Habakkuk 2: 3

For this I prayerfully hope.

Chapter 15

A Misunderstood Love

Daddy and Mother didn't date much at all before marrying. I'm not sure they should've ever married, but nonetheless, I was born within the first year.

My mother had an extremely hard time giving birth to me, and was pretty butchered up from having me. After I was born, the doctor threw me to the side chair and told my mother "she's not going to live". My grandmother didn't accept those words and picked me up, wiped me clean and held me close and loved on me. Because my Mom had such difficulty in childbirth, she had physical and emotional problems from this moment forward. Needless to say, I was an only child.

Life with my Mother was challenging to say the least. But, my Daddy was the very best dad in the whole wide world. I loved my Daddy and he adored me! And, my Mom knew it, but she didn't like it. Crazy, right? Daddy was a 'rough neck'. That's someone who works on drilling oil rigs. He worked long hours. So, most of my days were spent with my Mother. Normally, that's a good thing, except when you think that your Mother doesn't like you very much!

Had it not been for my Dad, I probably would have left home when I was old enough. But, hurting him was something I never thought of doing.

My Mom was pretty, extremely brilliant, played golf and tennis well, and was musically talented. I always thought she was so gifted. And then, there was me. It was difficult to feel good about myself, when I compared myself to her. I just didn't seem to ever measure up. We were direct opposites. She was a disciplinarian and liked her sense of order. I failed to meet her expectations and she used the 'switch' on me quite often as a child. I was thankful there were times when our trees didn't have any more low branches to use on me.

Because we were opposites, she didn't understand me. She yelled at me a lot and spoke ugly words to me, such as, "I wish I would've let you die when you were born, or I wish that I never had you!" My Daddy didn't ever hear her speak these words to me and I never told him. She rarely said hurtful things in front of him. It would've hurt him too much! I cried to my best friend and my high school boyfriend when my mother would yell and be mean to me. I didn't understand how a mother could treat her child the way that she treated me and yet, claim to love me. It was confusing! Her negativity hurt me and embarrassed me in front of my friends. When I was in Jr. & Sr. High School my relationship with her was especially difficult.

I stayed away from home as much as I could. I enjoyed being outside with the neighborhood kids, nine were boys and only one other girl. Because of this, we pretty much played boy games. I enjoyed being athletic and I also sang in the high school choir. My mother pushed me to play the piano and I hated it! I played until I was a junior in high school and had a bad experience at my recital and gave up the piano. I had a friend in high school who could play the piano beautifully. My mother would make comments about how much she must practice to play so much better than me.

I noticed that my Mother wasn't kind to me as my friends' mothers were to them. I tried to ignore it as much as I could, but deep inside I knew that our relationship was different. My friend's mother hugged me one day and said, "I don't know why your mother is the way that she is, but just love her."

When I was about 14 years old, she went to live with her grandmother in Ohio for a few months. I don't know why she went, but deep inside, I was happy she was gone. I enjoyed it when Daddy and I were at home together. My friends enjoyed coming to my house if my Daddy was home.

My Dad told me when I was in high school that my mother 'was not well'. If he went on the road for work, he took Mother with him. He knew not to leave us alone together. I would stay at the neighbors' house when they went away. The majority of my summers were spent at each of my grandparents' houses in

Oklahoma. I loved the time that I spent with them because I felt wanted. They were so kind and loving to me!

Life with my mother wasn't all bad. There were some days that we spent together shopping, or running errands that were fun and enjoyable! She didn't know how to love me emotionally, but she cared for me by cooking meals, and making sure I was clean, and she sewed nice clothes for me. Maybe those were days when she was feeling good and chose to be nice to me.

Mother and I always attended church, even though Daddy couldn't because he was working. Mother played the piano or organ in services and she taught a children's bible class. She was a wonderful VBS teacher! She could be so nice to other children, even though she wasn't to me most of the time. People in the church didn't know what life was like in our home. I was 9 years old when I professed my faith and belief in Jesus Christ and was baptized. My relationship with God made a big impact in my life. I spent a lot of time reading the Bible and praying.

Because my Daddy was so loving, it was easy for me to love God. He was my anchor. When he retired, he was able to attend church weekly with us. He enjoyed helping in the nursery, because he loved little ones. And, they loved him too! He had such a kind heart.

Although, my Mother didn't connect with me emotionally, she loved my Daddy! She was jealous that he loved me so much! I know that sounds somewhat crazy! I knew deep down that Mother loved me, but, I felt like she didn't like me. Maybe it's best to say, that she didn't understand me because I was different than her.

Ironically, when I was 18, I ended up marrying a man who continued to berate me as my Mother did. I endured it for 24 years until I left him. I'd finally had enough of his emotional and mental abuse! I knew that I could survive on my own.

Years later I moved back home to help out when Daddy was diagnosed with cancer. I was happy to help care for him. When it got really bad, he was put on oxygen. Mother would get mad when he wanted to stay up and wait for me to get home from work, so he could hear about my day. This is how I picture God. He longs to hear from His children, and he waits patiently, until they come home. My Daddy was always interested in my life. I enjoyed sharing my day with him. He gave me a reason to be excited to go home.

After several years of being back at home, he had a stroke and ended up in the hospital. My mom, and my uncle and I were there with him. We knew he wasn't going to make it much longer. I was holding his hand and I told my mother to come over and sit close to us, but she wouldn't. I said it again, but she still wouldn't come. I couldn't understand why she kept her distance. I wanted to love on him in his last moments and I wanted that for her as well. Shortly afterwards, he passed on. He looked so peaceful. It was then that I felt like he had taken me to the windows of heaven. I was at peace when his spirit departed. I knew then, that God was going to help me deal with the loss of Daddy.

Back at home, after he had passed, Mother spent weeks sleeping in Daddy's bed at night. I could tell she missed him. She knew he had been such a good Christian man. She told me, "I'm not going to heaven, because I'm too mean." I told her, "God was a forgiving God, and that he could forgive her if she asked". But, what I didn't say was that I had forgiven her. I wasn't ready. God was still working on my heart.

I continued to live with my Mother for 18 more years. I had a nice job working in the office at the university. Before she died, she said, "I could never understand you or how you got the job positions that you held, because I didn't think you were smart enough, but I guess you were." Those words, even though I was a senior citizen myself, were comforting to hear from her. In her own (negative) way, she was complimenting me. I don't remember her ever saying that she loved me as a child. My Daddy and my grandmother told me, "Your mother does love you". When I was caring for her I started telling her, "I love you" the last two years of her life, every night. She eventually said those three words back to me that I longed to hear my entire life.

The last five days I witnessed a miracle when they took her to hospice. Her heart softened towards me. I had finally experienced love from my mother. She wanted to give back to me and to others who visited her. She wanted to pray for them and not vice versa. It was quite touching!

Looking back, I don't regret for one minute being there with my Mother those 18 years after Daddy died. God knew that I needed all of those years to soften my heart towards her. And, the last two years, she became totally dependent on me. Oh, those were some tough and trying times! But, God was working on her with accepting and forgiving herself. And, more importantly, He worked on me during those years too! When I read the Bible, he taught me to depend on Him, and reminded me that He loved me. When my Daddy and Grandfather were alive, it was easy for me to understand and know God's love, because I saw such love in them. Not only for me, but for other children, and for people in general.

For years, I blocked the pain of the lack of love from my Mother, because it hurt to believe that she didn't care that much about me, her one and only child. When I had two children of my own, I experienced what it was like to be a mother. And in my eyes, motherhood wasn't what my mother gave to me. I never wanted my children to experience the 'mothering' that I had. But, having children reminded me of what I didn't have as a child growing up with her. It taught me to love my children with words of affirmation and to show it in my actions. Her seemingly lack of love for me was difficult to fathom once I became a Mother.

You would think as you grow up and become an adult, those feelings would 'grow' away, but they don't. And, even though there was healing between my Mother and I, I'll still never understand why she treated me the way she did. And, you know, I never did ask her why she treated me that way. I'm not sure she even knew why, or how to be different. I'm sure it was confusing and frustrating for her to understand. They didn't have the help for those who were chemically imbalanced back then, as they do today. I believe she wanted to be better, but she just didn't know how.

Being with my Mother all of those years, helped us bring healing to our relationship. If she would've asked me if I wanted to come and live with her for 18 years, I probably would've said, "No". But, God gave us the time that we needed to mend what was broken. She died with total peace. And, God knew what he was doing by having me care for her, because the Spirit softened my heart towards my Mother and gave me peace also. If Mother would've died before Daddy, I'm not sure that I would've had this peace. I needed to be the only person that she had left in the world, to care for her. God orchestrated her later years, so we could both find peace.

If you've grown up with an uncaring mother, I encourage you to find forgiveness and healing for the loss that you've experienced. Un-forgiveness is a prison. It's not a healthy place to be. Maybe you can't do it now, but there's still something that you can do in the meantime. You can grieve the lack of relationship you had with them. You can turn it over to God and read His Word to help you through the tough times. As a Christian, I think I know what's best most of the time, but I've discovered that God's way is best! God has been and is, my safety net. I know my God is big enough to take care of anything! I have experienced His grace and love in my own life. Because of Him, I was able to do things that I never thought I could. He has shown up in my life many times. He has been my Guide.

I've been comforted with His words in Psalm 139

> *O LORD, you have searched me and known me!*
> *² You know when I sit down and when I rise up;*
> *you discern my thoughts from afar.*
> *³ You search out my path and my lying down*
> *and are acquainted with all my ways.*
> *⁴ Even before a word is on my tongue,*
> *behold, O LORD, you know it altogether.*
> *⁵ You hem me in, behind and before,*
> *and lay your hand upon me.*
> *⁶ Such knowledge is too wonderful for me;*
> *it is high; I cannot attain it.*
> *⁷ Where shall I go from your Spirit?*
> *Or where shall I flee from your presence?*
> *⁸ If I ascend to heaven, you are there!*
> *If I make my bed in Sheol, you are there!*
> *⁹ If I take the wings of the morning*
> *and dwell in the uttermost parts of the sea,*
> *¹⁰ even there your hand shall lead me,*

and your right hand shall hold me.
[11] *If I say, "Surely the darkness shall cover me,*
 and the light about me be night,"

[12] *even the darkness is not dark to you;*
 the night is bright as the day,
 for darkness is as light with you.
[13] *For you formed my inward parts;*
 you knitted me together in my mother's womb.
[14] *I praise you, for I am fearfully and wonderfully made.*[a]
Wonderful are your works;
 my soul knows it very well.
[15] *My frame was not hidden from you,*
when I was being made in secret,
 intricately woven in the depths of the earth.
[16] *Your eyes saw my unformed substance;*
in your book were written, every one of them,
 the days that were formed for me,
 when as yet there was none of them.
[17] *How precious to me are your thoughts, O God!*
 How vast is the sum of them!
[18] *If I would count them, they are more than the sand. I*
awake, and I am still with you.
 English Standard Version (ESV)

Chapter 16

A Broken Heart

By Holly Sue Neeley

"Your Son has something called, Hypo Plastic Left Heart Syndrome. He will have a series of three open-heart surgeries to help him live with the heart that he was given and then eventually, a new heart. I want you to know that this is a lot for you to understand right now, but what you need to know is this will be a long journey for your family."

I remember the words as they hit me that morning. I can still see her face and her lips as she spoke those words. In that moment of feeling raw I wondered how she handled coming to work day in and day out telling hard news to families. I will never forget her face. She will forever be the face of that moment. Her eyes were kind and her face was gentle but her lips were drawn as she tucked her bottom lip over her top lip. As she began to talk I knew that what was happening couldn't be reversed, as if I was a different person before entering the door marked, FAMILY CONSULT ROOM. When she was finished talking she asked us if we had any questions. My response was calm, "Can we see him?"

Our son was just 15 hours old and I felt empty without him tucked safely inside my womb. I was mourning the person from the day before that was so filled with the excitement of having a son. All of our dreams of taking him home, his tiny shoes, and his first birthday all seemed to be fading and gone. I wasn't mourning him, but the life that we had dreamed about and the story that we had created in our heads. It all seemed to fall away and the reality seemed to be pressing our hearts from every angle.

As we neared the Pediatric ICU we were greeted by a couple of people in long white doctor coats who led us to our son. As soon as

I saw him I laid my arms and head over his little body and wept. Being a first time mom I had no idea how it felt to love someone like I loved him. It wasn't at all as I imagined it to be, it felt fragile and very scary. My son was diagnosed with a broken heart, but it was mine that fell in a thousand pieces.

We moved into our own space on the Cardiac ICU floor where they prepped and prepared us for his first surgery. We spent the majority of our time with him, only breaking to eat and sleep. We wanted him to feel us near and we desired to feel him near to us. Although he may not have recognized our presence those first nine days, we were near. I remember the night before he went into surgery; we went into his room and prayed with him as we had done every night. My husband prayed, "We ask that you heal our son, but even if..." Those words hit me hard, "but even if..." I felt the power drain from my body, that hard place of thanksgiving and joy in the midst of brokenness, hopelessness, and a fragile heart. My brokenness was now exposed and the power I thought I possessed to control my hearts condition fell to the floor with my tears. I felt helpless because I couldn't change it, I wasn't the source of the power. My letting go and my ability to allow myself to be broken was the start of understanding, "But even if..." I had professed that I believed this statement and I had felt very confident that when faced with a situation that I would in fact be unshakable. But until this moment, I had never experienced a "but even if..." situation, not one that was so hard to let go of.

That night our son, who rarely was awake and present, looked into our eyes. Leeland, in that moment, knew we were with him. It was in that moment that he saw us, he really saw us there. It was in that exchange of parents being seen and the child knowing that I realized God had been doing the same thing with us. He had been standing there, never-leaving, never-moving, stable and strong legged; as my son looked into our eyes, I truly was overcome with peace in knowing that God was there, even here and even if.

'A God that came near' was now my definition of hope. Hope was transformed for me that day. If He was near and if all He wanted for me was to know that He was near, I could stand with hope because the gap was closed. The power that was drained from our hearts was replaced with a peace of knowing the ever-present love of God. The nearness of him was almost tangible, because there was nothing else to be sure of. That feeling of nearness was love and His love felt powerful and His love was unshakeable.

That next morning we traveled to that familiar room and we thanked God for the hands of our surgeon. We hugged our boy one last time, kissing his perfect little chest and handing him over to be broke open and repaired. Why did life have to be broken? Why did saving his life look so much more like breaking him down? I was holding on, white knuckled, to the hope that I had discovered just 12 hours ago. I wasn't sure it was enough for Him to be near because today, Leeland seemed so far. Yesterday, I felt strong because the awareness of God's nearness was directly connected to Leeland seeing me near to him. Today that relationship seemed broken. This was that "even if..." we had prayed about earlier. Can I feel the presence of God even if Leeland doesn't survive open-heart surgery? Can God show me he's there even in the absence of my son? That day I had to surrender those questions and even let go of what could happen. I had to let that day happen and have faith that all of my experiences with God would pull the strength I needed to be alive that day. The greatest thing was that day, I had hundreds and hundreds of people standing with me. God orchestrated people to stand with me to give my legs the strength to face that day. I saw a few, but I heard of the crowds of people that were advocating for my son in prayer and gathering all over the world. It was that day that I knew I wasn't the only one that loved my son. The power of being loved was restored in the people that stood with us that day. God had once again showed me that He would show up, and today it was in the faces of His children.

We had spoken with several nurses about what to expect when we saw him for the first time after surgery. I'm not sure anything could've really prepared us for what we were about to see. His little body looked even smaller underneath all of the tubes, and cords. He laid so still, as a machine forced the air into his lungs. I was thankful that the doctors were so happy with the procedure, but I could see that the road ahead was long. Today was a good day, so we celebrated.

I remember a good friend that stopped in to see us just hours after his surgery. As he stood over the body of our little boy he said, "He trusts you. He trusts you with him." He said it with a half smirk as if he had seen this very thing before. And really, he had seen it thousands of other times, where the bad things aren't all bad. God is in the business of flipping the very bad into His very best! You could sense his excitement, almost as if he could see past this and further.

We knew it was hard, we knew it was scary, we knew God was with us, we felt God's love for us, we just hadn't thought about how God had actually gifted us with him in a way where it was chosen. Those words sunk deep into the layers of my very heart, the heart that I fear needed the actual work done, the heart that needed healing and repair. God had chosen me for this work. Although this was very new to us it wasn't new to God, he trusted *me* to take care of him. I had been praying all this time for God to heal my son and God was saying to me, "No child, he is my son and I know him well. I have brought him to you and I trust him to you. Love him the best that you can and care for him in every way that I have shown you care." I had it wrong the whole time, God trusted me with him, instead of me trusting God with him. I was wrong because he wasn't ours. When I realized that he wasn't mine I was able to love him deeply. I was able to care for him, because I knew the care that God had given to me, and I could do this one thing for Him. That day was pivotal for this journey. I felt honored to be Leeland's chosen mother. I vowed to care for him and love him for however long God granted me the time and I considered it a gift. That day when I felt so alone without Leeland in my arms, when I doubted because I felt empty while he was in the operating room, God had him and God had me. He's the only reason the relationship works, "He is in all things and in Him all things hold together." I knew that to be true, but I knew it now in the midst of all that I was learning. God gave, God came near, God loved, God provided and in that "even if", God is enough.

"If I rise on the wings of the dawn, if I settle on the far side of the sea, even there your hand will guide me, your right hand will hold me fast." Psalm 139:9-10 NIV

Chapter 17

The Fight of a Lifetime

I grew up in a large family, living a very normal life. My parents worked hard to instill in all of us family values and work ethic and above all, a love for God. I was in the "younger" set of siblings, being next to the youngest of 6 kids. We grew up as a very tight knit family and have made great memories over the years. I enjoyed being taken care of by my older siblings and looked up to them very much. In our lives up to that point, we had never experienced any major hardships or tragedies. We lost people we loved over the years, but they were older and had lived full lives, so it didn't seem so tragic. So when these turn of events came out of nowhere, it truly did rock our world and everything that we believed in and knew.

My oldest sister was 25 years old when things started changing. She had graduated college, married a Christian man and had just moved to Kansas where her husband was stationed for the Army. Not long after the move, she found out she was pregnant. She was delighted and more than ready to start a family and become a mother. As the pregnancy wore on, however, she began having pain in her back. She went to the doctor, but because of her pregnancy, there was not much they could do. Some thought maybe the pain was related to the pregnancy. She endured the pain and learned to deal with it privately because she was not one to bring attention to herself or tell people when she was hurting. In April 1988, she gave birth to a son and was on top of the world and the rest of the family was ecstatic. I remember getting the call from her after she had the baby. Long before the days of cell phones, my parents had received the call that she was in labor and started driving the almost 5-hour trip to get to the hospital. She gave birth before they were able to reach her and I was one of the first phone calls she made to tell the news. I was 16 at the time and my 14 year old sister and I had stayed behind to go to school and take care of things at the house. I knew she had been having some pain, but had no idea how bad it really was. Hearing the excitement in her voice and how happy she sounded, I clearly remembered thinking that the pain must be gone and it was completely related to the pregnancy; now that she had the baby, all would be well. The following day my parents returned home and I was shocked to hear them say that she was not doing well at all. They said she was in tremendous pain and could hardly walk down the hall. They returned home due to work commitments, leaving her in the hospital as the doctors would run tests and hopefully figure out what was causing the pain and "fix it." My parents seemed very concerned, which in turn concerned me. But, being a typical teenager and busy with school and activities, I went about my life not dwelling on it too long.

Three days later, I remember I had been at a school activity in the evening. I was running for president of an organization and ended up being elected. I was pretty excited because I had won and was coming home to tell my parents. I walked in the door and saw my Mom sitting on the couch crying as she was folding laundry. Of course, she immediately asked me how it went, but I knew something was wrong and I didn't care what was going on with me! She told me that my sister had been diagnosed with cancer. My sister was distraught and shocked and just didn't know how to call and tell my parents without breaking down. So she had called the preacher of our church and he came over to break the news to my parents.

Here's the reality my sister was dealing with: At age 25, four days following the birth of her first child, she got the news that the pain was directly related to cancer. She was diagnosed with Neuroblastoma--a rare childhood cancer--always fatal and seldom seen in adults. Doctors told her that there were only six documented cases before her and none had given birth. The prognosis was very bad, less than six months to live. The tumor was on the adrenal gland and had spread throughout her body. Surgery was not possible because of the location of the tumors.

The doctors fitted her with a back brace and scheduled treatments to help decrease the pain and try to shrink the tumors.

You can imagine the shock we were all in! We just didn't even know how to react. My aunt died from cancer a decade before; my Grandpa died from it as well, but this was so different. She was so young and had just had a baby!! My parents were in a different situation than most their age. They had three adult children who were married and had families of their own living in various locations. They also had a son in his first year of college in another state, and two daughters still in high school. They were both working full time and still raising kids at home. My Dad was an elder in the church and a volunteer firemen and had a mother in her 80's he needed to keep up with. My parents literally packed up that evening, sent us to stay with my sister and her family a few miles away and they headed back to see my sister and help wherever they could.

My parents were only able to help so much due to the distance and having jobs and family responsibilities. From the very beginning we saw God working in this awful situation. A woman whom my sister had begun a friendship with at church immediately stepped up and volunteered to watch the baby anytime day or night. She was such a blessing to my sister and her family! She had kids of her own, but rearranged her house, making one room into a nursery and took on the fulltime job of raising my nephew. She felt she needed and wanted to help my sister who couldn't even pick up her own son due to the extreme pain she was in. There was no way she would be able to care for a newborn baby and use all of her strength to fight the cancer in her body. She took care of the baby and was flexible anytime she wanted to see him. She talked daily on the phone with my sister, sharing all that was going on in the baby's schedule and anything that was changing. I just can't imagine all that was going through my sister's mind! How awful to just give birth and not even be able to take care of your child and at the same time have to fight for your life, not knowing what was going to happen!

For many months, she had to endure much hardship:

- Radiation beyond the maximum limits.
- At least six different types of chemotherapy
- Multiple pain medications
- Numerous steroids and muscle relaxers
- Side effects from the treatments and drugs
- Pain
- Lack of freedom due to drugs, tests, treatments, and doctors' appointments.
- She also had to deal with the continuous onslaught of bad news:
- Told by different doctors that the end is near or that it has spread to another part of the body.
- Told they cannot remove the primary tumor.
- Told they cannot give her the bone marrow transplant, which is the best hope.
- Told that this or that treatment is no longer effective.

All of these things were definitely a hardship on her and her family. She was always very independent and hardworking and did things herself. She had to spend lots of time in and out of the hospital. She had to rely on family members, and church members to help her with everything from getting to and from appointments, to doing things around the house and preparing meals.

An amazing thing about my sister is that she had a strong faith in God and an iron will and determination to live. I know her determination to live was because she wanted her son to know and remember her. I am so proud to say that she surpassed her prognosis by 7 years! It was a battle that took many twists and turns, where she encountered many ups and downs on her journey. During those seven and a half years, although her cancer was never officially in remission, God blessed her with several reprieves from the daily burdens of active cancer. She became an inspiration to me as well as countless others. She tried to live as normal a life as possible and raise her son to the best of her ability. She took up quilting, taught a bible class entitled "facing your own death" and wrote an article for a magazine about her experience with cancer. She also spent time with friends and family as much as possible.

I truly don't think I ever could empathize with my sister until many years later. As I had kids of my own and approached the age she was when she died, it finally "hit" me. I understood a lot more of what she had been through and all that she had to learn. Looking back over those 7 ½ years, I see many "miracles", many prayers answered, the sacrifice of my parents, especially my Mom, church members coming together to help, changed attitudes, faith strengthened and lessons learned. She truly was an answered prayer. When she was first diagnosed as having cancer, it was all over her body. They told her to get her life in order because she would not be here in a year. It's amazing that she lived 7 ½ years after her initial diagnosis. There was no physical way she could survive that long-but she did! I believe God sustained her because there were things she needed to do!

The most important thing I learned from my sister's bout with cancer is how temporary our life on earth is. Nothing is promised tomorrow. Life is NOT fair and that unexpected, even tragic things happen to good people. I learned that it's ok to question and struggle with your faith. It's ok to even be angry at God for a period of time while trying to make sense of a situation. My sister did lots of journaling during her down times. I saw on paper all of her fears, struggles and questions. I saw her anger and sadness, disappointments, thankfulness, joyfulness, contentedness and finally her faith in God being strengthened.

I used to have periods of feeling sorry for my sister and her situation. I would question why MY sister had to go through all she did. Why did she have to die and others be allowed to live? I felt like her situation was so unfair and why did she not get to see her son grow up, or have a "normal" life like other people? But one day, God allowed me to see that she truly is the winner! Her faith has now become sight and she is in a better place. God used her life to encourage others that were dealing with cancer. Her life helped her own family develop a stronger faith in God. She touched the lives of many people, including the friend who helped raise her son while she was getting treatments.

Over 20 years has gone by since my sister lost her battle to cancer. My kids have never met her, but I talk about her frequently. I want to make sure they know who she was and the impact she had on me and others. Her son is now married and has a son of his own. What's great is that we all have hope-hope that her life was all part of God's plan and that we will see her again in Heaven! As my Dad always says, *"What a day that will be!"*

Chapter 18

Skies of Hope

Being two weeks overdue, I was overjoyed to finally be gazing into my little girl's blue eyes. All was perfect at this moment. I was blessed to be married to John, a wonderful godly husband, and father to our 2-year-old son, Matthew and now, to our sweet baby girl, Dorie. She was a big baby. She was breach during the delivery and the doctor tried to turn her with forceps, but was unsuccessful. So, she entered the world from a caesarean section. I had endometriosis after John and I married and was told that I couldn't have children. So, you can only imagine how overjoyed we were to have two children!

One day as I was looking at Dorie, I noticed that she wasn't turning her head as she laid on her side. It was at that precise moment when I realized that something was wrong with my little girl. When she was 3 months old, I found out that I was pregnant. Nine months after Dorie arrived, we were thrilled to welcome another little boy, Michael, into our hearts. It wasn't long until Michael caught up in size to Dorie and people thought that they were twins. When he crawled, she crawled. When he pulled up, she did too!

I didn't realize it at the time, but God gave us Michael, so soon afterwards to teach Dorie. He was a godsend and a blessing because he could teach her things that John and I couldn't. It was encouraging to see Dorie progressing. Maybe she was just a little slow and simply needed Michael to show her what to do.

However, when she didn't walk, when Michael did, we knew something was wrong and made an appointment at a children's hospital. At 2 years of age she started physical therapy. The doctors couldn't give us a diagnosis. It was frustrating! I wanted whatever it was to just go away. She had to be 3 years old before they could do testing on her. John and I were told that if she would've been severe, they could diagnosis her. Well, that wasn't comforting at all!

Waiting was very difficult when all you wanted was your child to get better! But, I was also raising a 6-year-old and a 14-month-old baby, so that helped to keep my mind occupied at times. Two little ones did keep me busy! John was strong and dealt with whatever came our way. He helped care for the kids and was very supportive. When he could go to the doctors with me he did. He was my anchor.

Dorie was finally old enough to get tested. The tests revealed that she had Cerebral Palsy. When I learned that she probably had it from birth, I was angry that the doctor hadn't discovered it until now. I thought of the missed opportunities that could've possibly helped her. I was in disbelief and believed that she was going to get better. When she was 4 years old, she only said one-syllable words, no sentences. She started speech and physical therapy. Speech therapy went on for years because she struggled with how to process her thoughts and say what she wanted to say.

Michael soon surpassed Dorie mentally and physically. It was obvious that something was wrong with her. People would make comments when they saw her and it would upset me that they could be so rude. They saw things that I guess I couldn't. Or, was it that I wouldn't? Could my denial be enabling her to not progress? Apparently it was true because a doctor told me that I would be her biggest handicap! Oh, the gall! Isn't it natural for a parent to help their child? "Let her try to do it!" he said.

After I picked up my wounded ego, I realized that I needed to treat Dorie as normal as possible. John and I decided to put her in the public school system as a preschooler. It took her longer to do things, so she didn't advance as quickly as Michael. But, she was advancing, and that's what mattered. As she grew older, it was challenging finding her gentle and compassionate doctors to care for her with Cerebral Palsy. God took care of us by sending us to the Children's Hospital near us. She had 5-7 doctors at a time; a neurologist, a psychologist, a social worker, a physical therapist, a speech therapist, an orthopedist and a family doctor. My days were busy taking the kids to school and taking Dorie to her some kind of appointment. John loved all the kids, but he adored his little girl. Oh, and Dorie loved her Daddy! I was thankful that I had him to walk with me on this journey. Together we were doing the best that we could for her and helping her to be as independent as possible.

When Dorie was 15, we decided to go to Texas for Christmas to be with John's family. We left in the evening, so it was easier to sleep, and so we could arrive by Christmas dinner. My oldest son, Matthew had been driving, but his Dad told him to stop and he would drive. It was minutes from being Christmas Day when our van was struck by a sleeping semi-truck driver in Memphis.

I was unconscious for four days and woke up to learn that my husband had died in the accident. My Mom, John's brother and a family friend had flown to Memphis to be with us. There were only two things that I remember hearing: Matthew, who was 17 years old screaming at the accident scene, "Mom, wake up!" and my Mom saying in the hospital, "I'll always stay by Dorie".

I had bleeding on my brain and was kept sedated and therefore, I was unable to make decisions. My Mom and family made them for me. Michael and Dorie were flown home. Matthew stayed at the hospital going back and forth between me and Dorie and making calls back home to keep people updated. It was several days after the accident before they flew my husband, John's body home.

At the time, Dorie remembered the wreck, but she didn't know that her Dad had died. Dorie's knee was injured in the accident and she needed to have surgery under the care of her many doctors at a Children's Hospital. Dorie ended up having knee surgery the day of her Dad's funeral. And, I was still in the hospital in Memphis unaware of what was going on. I came back home nine days after the accident. Friends from my home church drove down to Memphis and took me, Matthew and my Mom back home.

My Mom moved in and helped care for me. Dorie was still in the hospital for another three months. I wasn't able to go to see her right away, but when I did, she asked for her Dad. I didn't lie to her, but I said, "Dad's not here right now" and she accepted my answer. I wanted her to concentrate on getting better, so I waited several weeks to tell her that he had died in the accident. I finally told her when she was able to come home. I wanted to be with her

139

when she got upset or had questions. I was surprised that she accepted it much better than I thought she would.

Life was so busy at our house with home health staff visiting for both Dorie and me. She wasn't able to walk on her leg for 3 months. After the accident, I thought she had gotten better mentally, but the doctor didn't agree with me. They had found a fatty embolism that traveled through her blood stream. It's where tissue gets disconnected and floats around. It was another medical issue that Dorie endured.

Life was busy, and I didn't have time to process my grief of losing my husband. Dorie missed her Daddy. For nearly a year she didn't want to go anywhere because she was afraid to get in the car. Because of my own health issues and Dorie's I didn't have much quality time with the boys. I knew they were hurting, but they didn't want to talk about the accident. Matthew, my oldest had just graduated from high school. He also had become more involved with a gal who had shown him emotional support after the accident. I understand him being drawn to her, but she wasn't a good choice for him. A Mother knows these things! He did things that had his Dad been here, wouldn't have happened. We were all hurting! Satan was working overtime in our lives. It was hard to juggle everything and deal with everything by myself now!

One thing I asked of Matthew when he went out, was to "Come to my room and tell me when you get home". One night he decided not to tell me and I knew it was about 3:00 in the morning. He was playing with 'fire', but I didn't know what to do. Matthew and his girlfriend decided to leave for a few days together even though I disapproved. Her parents had given them some money to take their little trip. I told him "your Dad wouldn't want you to tarnish his good name, and he knows a lot of people where you're going"! I was very hurt that he blatantly disobeyed me. I was so frustrated! His 14-year-old brother, Matthew was at home watching the whole thing play out. I had to make some tough decisions. I finally listened to the advice of a friend who told me to "turn it over to God", and to "stop taking it back". I had tried to do it myself and I was making it worse. After I *gave it all* to God, I got a call from my cousin who asked if Matthew could live with him and his wife for the summer. God had a plan. When Matthew got home, I kicked him out for disobeying me and told him he was going to stay with family out of town for the summer.

He got a job, and they helped him see life clearer. And, the positive thing was his girlfriend was a few states away! One night a call came at midnight for him from his girlfriend. The next morning, my cousin laid $200 on the table along with the phone and an ultimatum, "You can call her and end it or you can take the $200 and go home". He picked up the phone and broke up with her. I was overjoyed and proud of Matthew! I knew God was at work.

My cousin had been saving my son's money for him that summer. Michael made a decision to go to a Christian college where he got a degree and found his wife. God handled it so much better than I could've ever done! It was hard for me to let go completely and not keep picking it back up. God made a way when I didn't know the way! This had to be God because I would've never thought of him going to stay with them for the summer. It was apparent that God was working.

Matthew was strong and faithful growing up! He took his commitment to God very seriously. He helped me get through the hard times, by not giving me trouble. Dorie was still going to public school and graduated high school when she was 21 years old. After high school, she got a cafeteria job wiping tables and making a little money. She was proud of herself, but not as proud as I was of her! Shortly afterwards, she enlisted and was accepted by a local community college to their Special Educational Student to Work Program. She earned her Associates Degree in five years.

Dorie excelled when I started treating her as normal as possible. It wasn't natural for me to do with a special needs child because I wanted to help her so much! I wanted her to fit in as much as possible. I battled the school system on her behalf and she eventually graduated. Dorie's now 38 years old and lives in special housing for handicapped young people. She's shown that she can take care of herself and her apartment and can live with a roommate. She's very friendly and not a stranger to anyone. Her brothers know that they have a special sister with a disability. 99% of her friends are from church. I have intentionally sheltered her from the evilness in the world. She still has a child-like innocence and loves and believes in people. She has grown so much more than I ever would've thought. Life has been a real struggle at times. I know that I could never have gotten through it all without God and the love of my family and of the church. I've learned that when I gave everything to God, my dark clouds went away, the blue skies opened up and God showed me *hope*.

Chapter 19

The Battle Is Not Mine

"Do not be afraid! Don't be discouraged by this mighty army, for the battle is not yours, but God's." 2 Chronicles 20:15

Unfair treatment has always been a close companion of mine, at least as an adult. Unfortunately, many people are broken and scarred from their childhoods. I made it through my childhood pretty well. I grew up with both parents raising me, and I made some lifelong friends along the way. No, my scars aren't from my childhood. The fires I've had to continuously walk through have been in my adult years because I was chasing love from men instead of recognizing that love had always been all around me.

I guess you could say I was asking for trouble when, because I was too shy to talk to guys at school, I started chatting with guys on the internet. My very first experience with chatting online was in 1998 when chatrooms were still new, and predators, who could pretend to be whomever they wanted, were out on the prowl looking to deceive unsuspecting children.

I was sixteen, but because of my shyness and over sheltered upbringing I was very naïve and trusting. I ended up chatting with a guy who said he was twenty-one, and even though he knew I was sixteen, he still pursued a relationship with me. He finally talked me into giving him my phone number, and after a season of talking on the phone, he told me one evening that his age was actually forty-two. By this point, I was already attached to him, and though I made attempts to stop talking to him, I would eventually cave.

I was seventeen when I met him in person. He did sexual things to me during his visit that made me feel obligated to marry him. Two months after his visit, he moved in with my mom and me, and we were married at the local courthouse three months later. I had just turned eighteen only 4 days before. There had been multiple warning signs that he had a very controlling and angry personality even before marriage, but I swept them all under the rug because I felt I was already stuck.

It wasn't long before all the abuse started. He physically, mentally, verbally, and emotionally abused me. The physical abuse wasn't as bad as the daily verbal and mental abuse, though. He'd go into a rage over the littlest things, and I spent years walking on egg shells trying to be perfect so as to not upset him. The truth was, though, he could have misplaced his keys or spilt something on the floor and it would still be my fault. When he'd get upset with me, he would call me horrible names and degrade me, making me feel lower than dirt. The most common phrase he used was, "F off and die B!" I would usually leave the house when he'd fly into a rage, and if he became upset at night, I would sometimes sleep in the car. One night in particular while sitting in my car, I remember looking up at the sky through tear stained eyes and screaming at God, "How can you be up there watching this and not doing anything about it?" I started to become an angry, hateful, suicidal person who lived in a darkened world of depression. By this point he had already manipulated me in many ways to keep me under his control and to keep my family and friends out of my life. I felt like I was all alone and there was no one who could help me.

Though my life was a nightmare, there was something positive that happened three years into the marriage that gave me a reason to live. I had a beautiful baby girl named Alana who needed me to be the best mom I could for her.

In the summer of 2005, after six years of marriage, the physical abuse escalated. I was awakened one night from hearing him scream from the living room hateful words directed at me. Then he came into the bedroom and started pushing me, saying if he couldn't get any sleep then I couldn't either. I sat up and asked him what his problem was, and then he did something he'd never done before – he spit in my face. I finished the night sleeping in the car. The next day we didn't talk to each other until he ran out of an item he needed that evening. He started screaming at me about it, so I drove to the store and purchased the item for him. When I returned home, I couldn't get back into the house because he had latched the screen door shut and there was no key to unlock it. He wouldn't answer his phone, and I didn't want to wake baby Alana, so I sat outside and cried, saying to myself, "I don't deserve to live like this!" He finally opened the door and let me back inside. I threw the purchased item down and started packing my bags to leave. While I was at my dresser getting clothes out, he threw me to the ground and started strangling me as he had done many times before in the past. This time was different, though, because while one of his hands was around my throat, his other was punching me in the arm repeatedly. I had the thought that he had forgotten he still had a grip on my throat and that I had taken my last breath. He eventually let go of my throat and started punching me with both fists before he finally stopped and walked away from me while repeatedly saying, "You've ruined everything." I found my glasses on the other side of the room, put them back on, and headed out the door. Miraculously he let me walk out, and I drove straight to the police. I was too scared to press charges because I was afraid he'd retaliate once he'd be released from jail, but I wanted to have a police officer escort me back to the house so I could collect up my things without being attacked by my husband again. Since it was so late at night, I was told to go to a safe place and call for an escort in the morning. When two officers arrived the next morning, they arrested my husband, saying it didn't matter if I pressed charges or not because the state was taking over. That was the day God rescued me, and I remember writing in my journal, "Am I really free?" The police officer taught me how to get an order of protection, and I was given a two-year order of protection.

A few weeks later I was told by someone from my husband's past that I was lucky because my husband had abused a lady in a past relationship so badly that she had to be hospitalized. I immediately thought about the night in the car when I was looking up at the sky and yelling at God. I realized that God had been protecting me the whole time because I was never sent to the hospital. About a month later, I had a very personal experience with God making His presence and love for me known, and I became stuck to Him like Velcro.

I thought the worst was behind me after coming out on the other side of six years in hell, but I was about to learn that the worst was just beginning and would continue on for over a decade.

145

Through the divorce, Alana, who was two at the time, was to go see her dad for unsupervised visits. It wasn't long after those visits started that Alana would come home with concerning behavior. I contacted DCFS and an investigator came to our house. The investigator decided after Alana spoke about her dad touching her privates that she needed to speak with professionals at the Child Advocacy Center (CAC). Alana did not speak up at her CAC interview, though, so DCFS determined the allegations to be unfounded. I was very hurt that nothing was done to protect Alana, and I went into a brief denial. It wasn't long before I called DCFS again, after Alana said more about her dad touching her privates, and, again, it was unfounded. I was told not to call DCFS anymore. Instead, I was to educate Alana about good touch and bad touch.

One Friday evening before Alana was to be picked up by relatives and dropped off with her dad for the weekend, I decided to read Alana the good touch and bad touch book that the CAC staff gave me. When I read about good touch – tickles and hugs, Alana giggled, but when I read about bad touch – private parts being touched, Alana put her hand down her pants and began fondling herself. I asked her how she learned to do that, and she said her daddy taught her. I freaked out. I started crying uncontrollably and called DCFS. I was spoken to very coldly by the lady on the other end, and she didn't seem to care. I called Alana's relatives who were to pick her up soon and told them what Alana had done and questioned what kind of mom would I be to send her into a lion's den and that I wouldn't be sending Alana to her dad's. Then I decided I needed to call the police because I knew her dad would seek their help if Alana didn't show up for a visit. I was told that I had to send her or I'd be arrested because he was her dad and he had rights too. I thought to myself, *And, I am her mom and I should have the right to protect her.* I hung up the phone feeling defeated and called her relatives back to have them pick her up. The worst part of it all, though, was the damage my reaction did to little Alana. It was a long time before she was open with me again about anything that transpired while she visited her dad. If she would let something slip, she would immediately shut down and refuse to say more. That was pure torture – to hear enough to know that something was not right, yet to not hear enough to do something about it.

Over the next year, Alana hadn't said anything else concerning, so I started to believe, for my own sanity, that maybe I overreacted and nothing bad had ever happened. By this point I had met someone else and was engaged to get married. While my fiancé and I were visiting his relatives down south, Alana stayed with her dad. When I arrived back in town I received a phone call from a Department of Social Services (DSS) investigator. The investigator told me that Alana's dad had taken Alana to speak to DSS to say I was a neglectful mom and my fiancé was a molester. The investigator went on to say that when questioning Alana about life at mom's house vs. life at dad's house, Alana said that her dad touched her privates at night when she was asleep by putting "medicine" on them. Alana also said that her dad bathed with her and that her dad only washed her hair and private area while in the tub. Alana said that these were secrets she wasn't supposed to tell Mommy. The investigator told me that Alana was not allowed to leave with her dad and was placed in a foster home. The investigator asked me if I had any concerns when Alana would visit her dad, and I told her about the DCFS involvement the previous year. I was reassured that Alana would never be unsupervised with her dad again. I believed what I was told and began to put my trust in people instead of in my God.

After three months of no contact between Alana and her dad, a DSS worker called me a few days before the big trial and said there wasn't enough evidence to go to trial and to prepare myself for Alana's dad getting his unsupervised visits reinstated. This happened during the summer when visits would last for a week straight. I was devastated and shattered by this news. I thought to myself, *they didn't have enough evidence?* Alana's dad had self-reported that he bathed naked with her. When the investigator looked into his background, she found he had a history of assaults and sexual abuse allegations from another state. Also, he was supposed to complete a psychological evaluation, parenting classes, psychosexual therapy, and an anger management assessment/program, but he refused. *How can this system let him get away with this? THIS is justice?*

I sought out an attorney to help me fight for Alana's safety. I remember telling the attorney that I felt this battle could be compared to the Israelites' battle to flee Egypt. Every time Moses went to Pharaoh requesting the Israelites, who were slaves for the Egyptians, to be allowed to go into the wilderness to worship their God, Pharaoh would refuse. Later, though, he'd change his mind after a plague from God would be sent against the Egyptians. I imagined that the Israelites would find relief in leaving their enslavement behind as I would find relief in knowing that Alana was finally safe. But, inevitably, Pharaoh would again refuse, and I imagined the Israelites would feel disappointment and heartache as I would feel when I would be told to send Alana back to her dad. This pattern of refusal, plague, agreement, and back to refusal again continued for some time, and I imagined the Israelites got to a point where they stopped believing they'd ever be released, as I started believing no one would help Alana remain safe for long. The Israelites even had more impossible work demands put on them because Moses kept going back to Pharaoh, so I imagined they felt bitter at the injustice they were experiencing as I felt with my battle. I knew how it ended for the Israelites, though: God rescued them from their slavery in a miraculous way and brought Himself glory through it. That is what I put my hope in; God would eventually put an end to the back and forth safety and bring Alana into a permanent safety in a way that would be miraculous and would bring Him glory. The attorney believed I was being vindictive because the allegations had been unfounded, so she refused to fight my battle for me, and I began representing myself.

I found out a couple months after Alana started seeing her dad again that he had requested a review of the investigation and that meant having a teleconference with DSS's Child Abuse and Neglect Review Board (CANRB). During the teleconference I was asked to address my past concerns which would now include a discussion I had with Alana about how the "medicine" was put on her privates and how she said it was put on for a really long time. A few weeks after the teleconference, I received a letter in the mail from the CANRB. It stated that the investigation resulted in a Preponderance of the Evidence finding that Alana's dad was the perpetrator of abuse. As a result, his name had been entered into

148

the Central Registry. I had renewed hope that God's timing had arrived, and I felt relieved. Alana's dad appealed the CANRB's decision, however, and when he was summoned to discuss the matter in front of a judge, he told me that Alana would have to be a part of it. Instead of asking to see evidence of the request, I allowed him to take Alana to the court date. Not long after, I found out he had won his appeal, which meant the allegations were no longer to be spoken of, as if what Alana said never existed. It's hard to fight when you feel so defeated. I had lost all hope that the system would ever be able to help me keep my daughter safe.

One night, as I was tucking Alana into bed, she said, "There's nothing you can do and there's nothing I can do – it's up to Jesus." I was amazed to hear such truth come from my young one's mouth, but I was not yet able to fully trust Jesus with the battle for Alana's safety. Many people, even Christians, would tell me that I wasn't fighting hard enough for her, that I needed to do this or say that. My focus was still on fighting the battle out of my own effort.

When time would pass with Alana not voicing any concerns, I'd bury my emotions and live in denial. One day when Alana was seven, my buried emotions were brought to the surface again. I was receiving help from a local ministry that would have me watch educational videos in order to receive baby care items for Alana's baby brother. On this day I was to watch a video about child sexual abuse. Watching the video really upset me because I remember a part in it where the person said to pay attention to the signs of sexual abuse and that you can do something about it. I was angered by that because my reality was that every time I tried to do something about it, no one would help. Back at home, Alana could sense something was wrong and asked if I was okay. I told Alana that I watched a video I didn't like because it reminded me of things she had told me in the past and how I wanted to help her stay safe, but I couldn't. Alana told me that she couldn't do anything about it because she was just a child and that I'm the adult and I needed to do something. I broke down in tears and told her how I had tried over and over again to do something. I told her that it could stop if she told everything that had happened. She said she would tell me, and we went into her room to talk. She told me they were secrets her dad told her not to tell and she began backing out of talking because she was afraid he would get angry with her if she told. I told her I'd be there for her whenever she was ready to talk and that I loved her. Then I left her room and, in tears, started begging and pleading with God to help her talk. I wanted her safe already; I wanted His timing to happen already. Unfortunately, it was still not His timing.

Something that brought me peace and strength to endure through the pain was a thought I had while watching a true story movie. The movie was about a teacher who went through her own battle of injustice and how she wanted a student to speak up in court to help the truth to be known, but the student was too afraid to talk and refused to help. I could relate to the teacher's desperation of wanting the student to be strong enough to speak out against someone who had hurt them. I could relate to her feelings of hopelessness and defeat. Then I had this thought: it's not enough for *me* to want Alana safe; *she* has to want it for herself and be willing to tell anyone who needed to know. In the movie, the scared student went to the teacher and said, "I'm ready." I knew that was what I needed to hear from Alana.

Alana didn't voice anymore concerns over the next few years, and I buried my emotions and lived in denial again. When Alana was seven her dad started a custody battle. In court he was requesting full custody because he claimed I was not adequately caring for Alana, I was not spending enough time with her, I was bitter and acting in a manner that was detrimental to her, and I was verbally abusive to her. A Guardian ad Litem (GAL) attorney was assigned to the case to speak on behalf of Alana. The GAL wanted to meet with Alana twice - once with me and once with her dad.

Three weeks before the custody trial, I had to be in court for a separate matter. Alana's stepdad was being investigated by DCFS for physical abuse to Alana's little brother, and I was to be present at the initial hearing. Alana's dad was voluntarily present, along with his attorney, because he had received paperwork with dramatic wording that stated Alana lived in a household that could cause her death, disfigurement, etc. I knew that he had a very realistic chance of getting full custody of Alana now. The surprise for me, though, was seeing Alana's GAL attorney in the courtroom. I was confused as to why she was present when the initial hearing had nothing to do with custody.

The hearing started off with the GAL speaking first, describing how she went out of her way to be present because she had serious concerns about both of Alana's parents. She was concerned about my hesitation with filing for divorce. She said that she believed I was putting my own desires above the welfare of my children. She then began to list off "red flags" about Alana's dad: 1) Alana's dad was forty-two when he met me in an internet chatroom and continued to pursue me, though he knew I was sixteen at the time. 2) He married me four days after I turned 18. 3) The past issues of sexual inappropriateness from Alana's dad towards Alana were concerning. 4) One of her staff members who was a trained social worker said to her after one of her meetings with Alana that there was something not right with the interaction between Alana's dad and Alana when they were in the waiting room together. 5) When Alana's dad took her to meet with the GAL, Alana was dressed in a deep plunging V T-shirt, and the GAL said it was inappropriate because she could see Alana's little breast buds. 6) When the GAL asked Alana about her shirt, Alana said that her dad picked it out and that he said he knew it was a little big but that he liked the shirt on her. 7) Alana had mentioned to the GAL that there was a girl who lived in her dad's apartment building who she wasn't allowed to play with because the girl had been sexually abused, and when the GAL questioned Alana about her knowledge of sexual abuse, her response was that her dad would talk about it a lot. 8) Alana told the GAL that her dad would tell her stories of how her step-dad had sexually abused her but that she didn't remember any of it. 9) Alana also said during her meeting with the GAL that at her mom's house she would take a bath on her own and wash her own hair, but at her dad's house he still would bathe her and wash her hair.

The GAL concluded by saying she wanted Alana's dad, mom, and stepdad to get psychological evaluations. She said she didn't want to be in a courtroom with the child who was sexually or physically abused and that she wanted to stop it before it could happen.

Next, Alana's dad's attorney had his client take the stand. His attorney asked him if he bathed his daughter below the neck, to which her dad replied no. His attorney asked if he bathed her above the neck, and he described how he washed her hair for her. His attorney asked if there was any other part of her body that he bathed for her, and he said, "That's kind of a trick question." He said, "Sometimes he'd bathe her with a wash cloth because her vagina would always be rashed out and it would always smell". He said that he's kind of a nurturer and that the doctors would tell him he's doing a great job. He accused me of punishing Alana by making her wear the same pair of underwear for four days – this, he said, was the reason he had to assist with washing her vagina.

The judge decided that all the children needed to be placed in a foster home and that all parents involved would be getting psychological evaluations. When the judge stated his reasoning for removing the children from me, he said he was a little concerned about the vaginal situation and if there was an issue, he wanted to make sure that I would be able to take care of the proper things. I assumed that meant that as soon as DCFS could show from a medical standpoint that I was a fit parent, I'd get the children back. Oddly enough, I had a peace so strong within me that kept me from becoming a fretful mess about the children being removed. I was relieved to know that Alana was not going to be placed in the custody of her dad and that he was going to be evaluated. I believed that my children would be gone for no longer than two weeks. I was naïve to the steps the court takes when children are removed from the home; they were in foster care for almost a full year. After about a month without my children back, I became very bitter towards the GAL who spoke against me in court and towards Alana's dad for his blatant lies against me that became the reasoning for my children's removal. It took me months before I could find peace again because I had my eyes on the injustices: my children being removed from home when it was because of my concerns for their safety that the court even knew about the abuse, my job loss with the school district because they were afraid I'd paint them in bad light, and the stigma that people had against me because I was a mother who had her kids taken from her.

I seriously contemplated divorcing my husband, and the only reason I didn't was because one evening while I was begging God to make my husband a good dad for his kids, I had a revelation come to my mind: He will never be the dad I want him to be or the husband I want him to be until he becomes the man of God he's meant to be. I trusted that God gave me that revelation to help me believe that He was working on my husband's heart.

A few months after the kids moved into the foster home a concern was brought to my attention. While Alana, who was now eight, was on a supervised visit at her dad's, her dad told the case worker that he had "Friday night bath nights" for Alana and he wanted to have permission to bathe her. The case worker told the foster mom about it, which led to the foster mom having a conversation with all of the children about safety. Then she had a private conversation with Alana to ask her about "Friday night bath night." Alana revealed several things: 1) Alana's dad bathed her every night, not just Fridays. 2) He would wash her hair, body, and private area. 3) Alana was not allowed to take showers because her dad told her there wasn't enough hot water for one. 4) Her dad would always put gel on her private area and would tell her that she has "problems with her vagina" and "always has a rash." 5) Alana, when asked how the gel was applied, said her dad would put it on his two fingers and would put it on the outside and inside of her vagina. 6) When asked how long it took, she said sometimes it would take a long time. 7) Alana's dad would sleep with her on the sofa bed every night because there were too many clothes on his bed.

The foster mom said Alana had not had any rashes or issues with her privates while in foster care, so Alana's confessions were, in her opinion, of serious concern. She was hopeful that justice would be served this time, especially since Alana had agreed to speak with her case worker, her GAL, and a county investigator in a meeting set up by the foster mom. I, on the other hand, was not hopeful and expected the ball to be dropped as it always was in the past.

At the meeting, Alana recounted everything she'd told the foster mom. The foster mom was told to call the child abuse hotline, which put her in contact with DCFS. DCFS wasn't happy that Alana had spoken to others prior to speaking with them because it could taint the investigation and result in added stress for Alana. DCFS was also concerned that the reporting process had already taken too long.

Alana got set up to have an interview at the CAC. Later that day the foster mom called me and told me that after the interview Alana said she wasn't brave. DCFS determined the allegations to be unfounded because there was not enough evidence in the interview to indicate Alana's dad for sexual abuse. I was numb to the results, having never put any hope in the investigation in the first place. The foster mom, though, was devastated and shocked that a little girl would tell her secrets to professionals and still it wasn't enough to keep her safe. The foster mom wrote a letter and sent it to everyone who Alana confided in. The letter addressed the foster mom's concerns for Alana's safety, and how, at the very least, she hoped Alana's contact with her dad would remain supervised indefinitely. Everything Alana had spoken about was found in the letter also. The foster mom was trying to do what she could to help protect Alana, but the letter became a weapon used against Alana instead.

At one of Alana's dad's supervised visits, he took Alana into a bedroom and began reading the foster mom's letter to her. He had a copy of it somehow and cornered Alana with it, aggressively questioning her about its validity. The even bigger tragedy was that the case worker allowed for this behavior to occur on his watch.

A few months later at another court hearing, the judge found me to be fit, and the children were returned to me. My husband was also found fit because he had completed everything that had been asked of him, but I did not feel comfortable with allowing him to move back in with us yet, though he did eventually move back in again. Alana's dad, however, was found unfit because he had not completed any of the recommendations that came from his psychological evaluation - he was to attend parenting classes, trauma therapy, and complete a sexual perpetrator evaluation. The judge realized that those were not typical recommendations to stem from a psychological evaluation, and without Alana's dad following through with any of them, he was still seen as a risk to

Alana's safety. Later, though, her dad was set up with supervised visits through a visitation and exchange center.

At some point after the allegations against Alana's dad had been made, I received paperwork in the mail from the courts. Alana's dad was suing me for $100,000 stating defamation of character. He was also suing the agency that oversaw the supervised visits. He said we were all a part of locking Alana in a room at the foster home and that we wouldn't release her until she would tell lies about him. The lawsuit was thrown out without much effort.

Three months after the supervised visits started, Alana's dad took me back to court wanting his unsupervised visits reinstated. I turned in an eighty-seven page response to his petition stating three major reasons why unsupervised visits were not in Alana's best interest: 1) Alana's dad was still seen as unfit by the court, 2) Alana still had concerns with being left alone with her dad, and 3) her dad's behavior during his supervised visits was not always appropriate. I included a copy of the court order that found Alana's dad unfit and many other related items. I spent days upon days preparing my evidence to fight for Alana's safety, but any time I tried to speak truth to the judge, he cut me off and forbid me to talk. I knew I wasn't allowed to talk about the past allegations due to being unfounded, but I became frustrated when the judge had deaf ears to Alana's dad being found unfit. Also, the judge didn't seem to think Alana's dad's behavior at the supervised visits was inappropriate, focusing more on the most recent three months of supervised visits that her dad had completed without incident. The judge acted like Alana never said anything concerning because he believed DCFS wouldn't have made it unfounded if she had. At one point I told the judge, "Your honor, no matter what, my daughter's words will never be erased."

I knew before the actual trial that the judge was going to award Alana's dad his unsupervised visits again because the judge had hinted to it at a different hearing by saying that unless I had new allegations against Alana's dad, there was nothing I could do to stop it. I left the courtroom feeling angry, broken, and defeated. I went home and wrote out my emotions into a poem that was about what it feels like to be a mom with her hands tied.

Not long after Alana went back to unsupervised visits with her dad, her personality started to change. She became very negative and nasty toward me and her siblings. She often said to me that if she ever got to choose which parent to live with, she'd choose her dad.

One day, when Alana was eleven, a DCFS investigator came to my house. I assumed Alana's dad had made the call as he had done many times before. This time, however, I was informed that Alana herself went to a school counselor which led to DCFS being contacted. Hurtful lies had been said against me, and, though DCFS determined the allegations to be unfounded, I began to lose hope that I'd ever be able to keep Alana safe and that I may never have a good relationship with her. Through those feelings I wrote a song called "Possible With You." It was a way to express the hopelessness I was feeling but to also reaffirm my trust that God's in control. The song begins, "Well maybe I'm getting tired of fighting for someone who doesn't even want to stay. Well maybe I'm getting to the point where I'll stop trying. Oh, God, can you help me find a way to keep on believing the impossible is possible with you in control of my life? Won't you help me trust you and keep on believing the impossible is possible with you?" This wasn't the first time I used songwriting or poetry as an outlet for my emotions, but this was the first time through writing that I was reminded no matter how impossible things may feel, the impossible is very possible for the Creator of the universe.

When Alana was eleven, her dad and I finally had our custody trial. His attorney had recently gotten in trouble with the law and was no longer practicing, so both I and Alana's dad were representing ourselves. In the courtroom, the judge spent a lot of time reading through past documents in our court file and then finally spoke his determination. He said, according to state law, Alana wouldn't have a say to which parent she lived with until she turned eighteen. This was good news to me because it meant unless a judge took custody away from me, Alana would never be isolated with her dad, a fear I carried for years. The judge also said that there was no reason to take custody away from me and that he didn't want to see us in court again for a couple years. I had been going to court for almost nine years straight, so I was relieved that

Alana's dad would not be able to file anymore petitions for at least the next two years.

When Alana was twelve, I started a part-time job working with senior citizens. The organization I was working for had me watch a mandatory video that was all about child sexual abuse. It was extremely difficult to sit and listen to perpetrators talk about the tactics they would use to groom children and to listen to former victims talk about abuse they had experienced as children. Everything I had buried deep inside of me was resurfacing yet again, and I remember thinking how I had to do something. I had the thought of contacting a parent of one of Alana's friends to find out if any type of abuse had happened to Alana's friend, but I never contacted the parent.

That night, after all the kids were in bed, I sat on the couch in darkness and started talking to God. I spoke to Him differently than I ever had in the past – no begging, pleading, or bargaining this time. It had been eight years since Alana told me that her rescue was up to Jesus, and I was finally ready to surrender. I simply said, "God, I'm not going to do a thing about this except put it in your hands. I'm letting go and trusting you to keep my baby girl safe because after years of fighting this battle as hard as I could, I have not been able to keep her safe out of my own effort. I'm no longer going to sit back and bury this inside me as if nothing ever happened. I believe her words, and I know you love her so much more than I could ever love her, so here. This battle is yours, not mine. I am going to come to you every night like the persistent widow and make my requests to you. I request that you rescue Alana from harm and keep her safe. I also request that justice is served and Alana's dad will get the consequences for his actions that he's supposed to receive. But just as Paul was out harming Christians and you had mercy on him, flipped his life upside down, and transformed him from the inside out to become a Christian himself, I believe you can do the same for Alana's dad. I don't just ask this of you because it would keep Alana safe and make our lives easier, but because it would bring you glory. I mean, how many people can't stand this man? Just think how much they'd all be in jaw dropping awe at the change they'd see in him when you'd fill him with your love and your kindness. Thank you for carrying this burden for me and listening to my requests. I love you. Good night, my God." I didn't bring those requests to God *every* night, but I did make those requests several times, and about a month later, I started to see one of the requests come to fruition.

Alana had come to me and asked if I would take her dress shopping because there was soon to be a school dance. I drove her and her little sister Emma to a nearby town to find a dress. During the drive, the topic of Alana's new boyfriend got brought up. I asked her if she was still with him, and she said she was but not to tell her dad because he was under the impression that it was over. Then she started telling me of an incident that happened the week prior while she was at her dad's. She said her dad found a love letter in her binder and was furious that she was dating a "black boy." She said he got physical and pushed her down on the bed and started hitting and kicking her. I stayed quiet and listened. I knew contacting DCFS again would do no good if she wasn't willing to have the help for herself. When we arrived at our destination, I asked her if she wanted help and was willing to tell anyone and everyone necessary in order to get that help. She told me what I thought I'd never hear: "Yes. I'm ready."

The DCFS investigator came out to our house the next day and, after questioning Alana and seeing the marks on her, told me that it wasn't enough to keep Alana from going back to the next visit with her dad, which was in two days. *It's NEVER enough,* I thought to myself, feeling defeated yet again. *How can this system expect a mom to ignore her mother bear instincts of wanting to protect her young?* I had promised Alana that if she spoke up that she would get help. I was crushed by the investigator's words. Before leaving, though, the investigator told me we still had the right to get an order of protection (OP).

The next day we went to the police station and Alana spoke with an officer about the incident. The officer sent her out of the room and asked me if I believed her story. I told him I did, and he asked me why. I told him because I have been physically abused by that same man. The officer didn't seem to listen to me because he proceeded to tell me that he believed Alana was upset with her dad because her dad probably disciplined her for rebellious teenage behavior and she didn't like it, so she wanted to get him in trouble. I couldn't believe what I was hearing. Yet again any hope of help was slipping through my fingers, so I turned my thoughts to God and started silently asking: "Please, God, open this officer's eyes to see that Alana is telling the truth. Give him the mind to understand that this is serious, and work through him to help us. Thank you." Within minutes of taking what felt impossible and placing it in God's hands, the officer asked me what Alana's dad's name was. When I told him, he gave an exasperated sigh, and his attitude did a 180. The officer told me that he knew of Alana's dad well and even remembered being called to my house over a decade ago when I was the abused victim and Alana was a little baby. The officer took pictures of Alana's bruises, but he said with the bruises being about a week old, they didn't show up well in the pictures, so our evidence was weak.

After leaving the police station, we went to the courthouse to file an emergency OP. The same legal assistance group that helped me over a decade before with my emergency OP against Alana's dad was able to help Alana fill out the paperwork. When Alana and I walked into the court room to speak to the judge about granting our request, I was immediately relieved to see that the judge was Judge Riley, the only judge I felt who was fair and just at our county courthouse. He spoke gently and kindly to Alana and asked her if she wanted to stay away from her dad. She said yes, and the emergency OP was granted. What an amazing feeling of relief it was that Alana was getting the help she was finally ready to receive!

The attorney assigned to help Alana was very negative and discouraging when it came to hopes of getting a one-year OP granted. The emergency OP enforced there was to be no contact between Alana's dad and Alana, but it was only good for two weeks. After getting off the phone with Alana's attorney a few days after the emergency OP was granted, I felt so helpless and broken and believed that in a couple weeks she was going to have to go back into the hornet's nest again like always. My despondency didn't last long, fortunately, because I decided that if we only had two weeks of safety, then I was going to live as presently in the two weeks with her and with as much joy and peace as I possibly could.

Two weeks turned into months because every time we went back to court about the OP, it was continued for a later date due to criminal charges pending against Alana's dad. Her dad was not denying that the incident occurred, but he was changing the story, saying he only "charlie horsed" her and didn't cause any physical harm to her. He lacked remorse and acted as if *he* were the victim.

After a few months went by, I received a call from a detective who knew of my concern for Alana's safety because he was present at some of the CAC interviews in the past. He told me that a friend of Alana's had recently told the police that 4 years ago Alana's dad had sexually abused her. I was familiar with who the detective was talking about, not because I ever interacted with her, but because during the time when Alana was on supervised visits with her dad, he would show up to court with a young girl and would tell me he was taking care of the girl long term because she came from a bad family that couldn't take care of her. I was later told by a DCFS investigator that the girl's mom told the investigator that she would allow her daughter to go with Alana's dad for overnights because he claimed Alana wanted the girl to come over. This was not true, though, so the girl was being picked up to be isolated with Alana's dad. I was sick to my stomach when I heard this news. My thoughts went back to the day I had to watch the video about child sexual abuse and how I wanted to see if a friend had been abused by Alana's dad. Now I was finding out that indeed it had happened to a friend, but to a different friend than I had suspected.

Too much time had passed from when Alana's friend said the sexual abuse had occurred, so no criminal charges were brought on Alana's dad for the alleged abuse, but DCFS believed the girl was telling the truth and made an indicated report against Alana's dad.

After eight months of the emergency OP being extended, a judge finally granted Alana a one-year OP. By this time Alana's dad had pled guilty to physically abusing Alana and was given one year of probation. His plea that summer was finally a piece of justice. If only I would've known what else was going to happen that summer, maybe I could've protected my Alana.

160

I had just given birth to my fifth and final child, a second little brother for Alana. I was taking a nap while the baby and two-year-old were sleeping, and the rest of the family was watching a movie together – or so I thought. Not long after I had awakened, I heard a scream and went to investigate. I found Alana locked in the bathroom with her seven-year-old brother. When she unlocked the door so I could enter, she was very visibly shaken and scared. She refused to leave the room at first, but then finally she agreed to take a drive with me. I drove to the park, and as I parked the car, Alana told me that she and her stepdad had gone into a bedroom because she wanted to act out scenes from the movie they had been watching. By a certain point he did the unthinkable, and he threw everything away in that very instant – almost ten years of marriage, his family's trust, his relationship with the kids, everything. When he fondled her, she ran out of the room and locked herself in the bathroom. He followed behind her and tried to unlock the bathroom door, and that's when Alana screamed the scream that I heard and went to investigate. I was broken in a way I had never been broken before. I believed what my shattered and terrified daughter had told me, and I immediately drove her to the police station. She repeated the account to two officers, and they followed us home to speak to her stepdad. He was removed from the property, and I was to take Alana to the hospital.

I kept it all together and stayed strong for my kids' sake during the day, but that night I was an emotional wreck. I locked myself in a room and just pounded on the floor, screaming and crying, broken and betrayed. *How could he do something like this? After seeing me fight in court for years for Alana's safety, knowing that something sexually inappropriate was going on between her and her dad, how could he do the VERY thing in which I was trying to protect her from? How could he betray us all in such a horrific way? She trusted him. How could he DO that to her???* I was so angry and confused and hurt, and Alana was, of course, going through her own mixed emotions. I had to pull myself together and be there for her. She had been blaming herself for the incident, and I had to let her know that she did the right thing; she did NOTHING wrong.

161

Alana spoke about her dad's concerning behavior several times from the age of two to twelve. The agencies that are trusted to keep children safe proved to me to be faulty. Alana was brave enough to tell the secrets to people she trusted, and that should've been more than enough to be expected of a small child. But in order to be helped, there was a specific process that Alana had to go through, and if she wasn't brave enough to jump through all the hoops and save herself, as it felt, then those who promised to help keep her safe would turn their backs on her. The end result each time was that she was forced to go back into isolation with the one she needed protection from. This taught her that speaking up did nothing to help; it just let her dad know that she had told, which made her life even harder than it was before telling. If the agencies could have seen the red flags as Alana's former GAL attorney saw them, and if they would've believed in stopping the abuse before it happened as Alana's GAL spoke of in court when Alana was seven, then she could've been safe at age two, and Alana's friend would've never been sexually abused by Alana's dad. I am learning how to hand over to God my anger and replace it with forgiveness. I long for the healing of the scars that walking through the fires of injustice have made on my heart, and little by little God is bringing me healing.

Ten plagues struck Egypt before Pharaoh, the Egyptians and the Israelites would see the power of God through them, and, the Israelites be set free from hundreds of years of slavery. I went on ten emotional rollercoasters over a period of ten years before Alana was rescued. The Israelites were purposely led into a corner of the wilderness where they felt trapped by the oncoming enemy. That set the stage for God's miraculous rescue: the parting of the Red Sea. After Alana said she was ready for help, I felt backed into a corner three times: when the DCFS investigator said it wasn't enough, when the police officer said he didn't believe Alana, and when the attorney said the incident was Alana's dad's first offense and no judge would grant an OP. All three times, though, God "parted the Red Sea" and made a clear path to safety for Alana.

Currently, Alana's stepdad is serving his 5-year prison sentence. Alana still has an OP against her dad, though it ends in a month. The time I've had with Alana has strengthened our relationship, and we are very closely connected now. She has become someone even stronger and more admirable in my eyes. She does not let her past affect her future. She wants to be a police officer, and I have no doubt that she will achieve her goal. I believe God will work through Alana to make a difference in the lives of other children who are in dangerous situations and need a hero to rescue them.

The story doesn't end here. What will come once the OP expires is still unknown, but one thing is for sure – God is in control of the outcome, and though the battle may rage on, the battle is not mine. I have learned how to trust my God to do the impossible and to claim BIG! I have learned how because I have experienced his mighty works. When I tried to fight the battle for Alana's safety out of my own useless effort, the outcome would just worsen, but when I surrendered and handed it *all* over to God, I saw miraculous results. He truly has proven to me that the battle is not mine.

Chapter 20

Senior Blessings

"The Lord Is My Helper" Psalms 118:7

By Jonnie Carroll

I love being a wife and mother! God has given me the gift of care giving. I enjoy being with my husband and my boys. And, decorating my house with treasures I find at antique and thrift shops, and especially with my Grandma Dodo's beautiful artwork.

I learned about God from my mother's mother. Oh, how I loved spending time with her! Psalms 145:3-4 is one of her scriptures that reminds me of her, "Great is the Lord and most worthy of praise; His greatness no one can fathom. One generation commends your works to another; they tell of Your mighty acts." She did this for me by giving me a strong foundation, a "rock to stand on". Psalms 40:2

My mother lived five hours from me in the town that I grew up in. When she was 85 years old, she had hurt herself and had three compressed stress fractures in her back. When I spoke with her on the phone, I could tell she was in intense pain. Her pain made me uncomfortable, and I told my husband that I needed to visit and check on my Mom, because I didn't like what I heard on the phone. When I arrived I noticed that she was pretty bad off. I was happy that I had made the decision to make the trip to visit her. My plan was to stay with her as long as she needed me to, so I could help her get stronger. She was doing rehabilitation and was on morphine and hydrocodone for the pain. I stayed for a few weeks and she still wasn't doing well. After speaking with my husband, we decided that it was time for her to come live with us.

Eight years ago my mother moved down to my house from Rockford, IL. I told Mom, "I'm taking you home with me". She agreed that it was the best thing for her. A scripture that gave me great confidence and still continues to do so, is Isaiah 41:13 "For I am the Lord your (my) God who takes hold of your right hand and says, Do not fear; I will help you." It was time to start packing her up for the move. We needed to decide what to get rid of and what treasures she needed to keep. I knew we couldn't bring all of it with us. Getting rid of her possessions was actually fun because she knew and loved so many in the high-rise apartment she lived in. She would tell me who to take things to, and I'd deliver all of her stuff to people that loved her. It not only made her friends happy, but it made Mom happy too! I even sold some of her belongings right on the spot. It was an in-house yard sale. Her cleaning lady was extremely good to Mom. She was given many clothes, and it thrilled Mom to give them away to her. I knew that I wanted to decorate her 'new' room with familiar things that she loved and would help her to feel more at home. My husband drove up and helped me. I knew this was Mom's last move. She was pretty frail, so, my husband fixed up the back seat with blankets and pillows to help make her comfortable for the five hour drive. Then, we packed her up and headed home.

Naturally being in a new area meant I needed to get her new doctors. I found one in St. Louis and he made changes with her medication. He took her off her bone nose spray medicine. The doctor gave her 30 mg of morphine and hydrocodone then later upped it to 60 mg of morphine. She was only on 15 Milligrams of morphine in Rockford. I was surprised that he had raised it so much! Later, she developed a fever and began having hallucinations. She told me about people being on the ceiling, and they turned to her and smiled. She began clearing her throat and after a couple of days she had pneumonia. When we got to the emergency room, I said that she was on morphine. I was surprised when the doctor immediately took her off of it. It's highly unusual to do so suddenly, and I feared she would have reactions to it. But, surprisingly she was doing better. Again, God showed himself as the God who "longs to be gracious to you, He rises to show you

166

compassion" Isaiah 30:18. All through the eight years of caring for Mom this scripture was loud and clear! The doctor got her back into rehab and she continued to get better and better and I was able to bring her home.

Mom rarely would drink water. She might drink a ¼ cup for the entire day when she was in the hospital. When she got home she began swelling up. She also had congestive heart failure. I took her to the ER. She had an accident waiting to see the doctor, and she needed a change of clothes. I told her I would go home and get her some clothes before we admitted her to the hospital. She said, "No, please don't put me in the hospital again. (She had just gotten back home from her last hospital stay.) Take me home please". I talked to her some more about her needing to be in the hospital and she said, "No way! I'm not going back". So, I took her home. Mom's mind was good, and I gave in to her wishes.

It wasn't long before her body began swelling up again. A home health nurse came by and saw how she looked and said she needed to be in the hospital. She said, "No, I'm not going to the hospital". I prayed for her and she went to bed. The next morning she woke up, and said, she had sweat a lot. She was fine. She never had this problem again. God watched over her and saved my mom again.

I tried to get her to exercise she wouldn't do it. I tried to get her to drink water, but she would rarely do it. I'd tell her "Mom if you don't exercise you won't have muscles to move." She would get so aggravated with me at times. I only wanted her to do it for her health. I was very in tune with her symptoms. My frustrations were many because Mom would make bad decisions: she wouldn't eat right, drink enough water or exercise. I would make her come to the kitchen, instead of bringing the food to her room, just so she would get out of the recliner and move. Why did have to fight me so much! I was only trying to do what was best for her. A scripture God would bring to my mind was Philippians 4:5, "Ley your gentleness be evident to all".

Mom continued to lose more weight. She was down to 95 pounds. When she came to live with us, she weighed 120 pounds. She was always cold! That was probably because she had zero body fat! She would wear a sweat suit, and her room would be 80 degrees and she would still want a blanket on her. She also had a space heater in her room. She was beginning to show signs of dementia, so her reasoning was askew. She kept putting her blanket on the heater. I told her it could cause a fire. I had to take the heater out of her room because mold was also starting to grow on the walls.

There were many trips to the doctor during the eight years that she was with us. One time in the hospital there was a doctor that listened to me and treated Mom accordingly. God used that doctor a few years later to help me. Instead of them telling me what they were going to do, they asked me what they thought my mom needed. I know that that was God.

She was getting so bad and didn't have much mobility. She went to the hospital again, and then onto rehab. She continued to get worse, and I had to put her in a nursing home. She was very unhappy! She was there for a week and I cried every day. I was having such a hard time seeing her unhappiness, and her care was horrible, so I decided to bring her home. God allowed her to come home for a week, but then she got real bad.

She hardly had any strength and now I had to be at her side 24/7. My husband had recently had foot surgery, and I needed to dress his wounds. It was impossible for me to help him when I needed to be by her side, so I put her in a nursing home. There was a nursing home two minutes from my house but I'd heard nothing, but bad things about it. One day I stopped in at the local convenient store and ran into a friend that was a nurse. She just 'happened' to work at the nursing home that I had heard the bad things about. I asked her about the nursing home. She said, "A retired Army nurse was now running it, and it was going well". I knew that this was God working because He had given me a sign. I had tried to get her into that nursing home, but I couldn't get her in without a doctor's approval. I had fired her doctors, so I didn't know how I was going to manage getting her a room there without their recommendation. Once again, I had to take Mom to the ER. I called the nursing home to see about getting her admitted and was told the emergency room doctor could send her to the nursing home. The ER doctors didn't realize that they could do this until I told them what the nursing home told me. They got right on it and she soon had a room waiting. The scripture in Isaiah 63:7 tells exactly how I felt, "I will tell of the kindnesses of the Lord, the deeds for which He is to be praised, according to all the Lord has done for us. Yes, the many good things."

I had talked to the nursing home about putting Mom on hospice. I thought that they were taking care of it, but I hadn't heard anything. Mom was getting worse. She was losing more weight and was now down to 85 pounds. Mom's roommate was on hospice, so when the hospice nurse came in the room and took a look at my mom, she got her on hospice right away. God was taking care of Mom!

After two weeks on hospice, it was obvious that Mom was dying, so they gave her morphine to help ease her anxiety and allow her to relax. Every single second I wanted to do what I could to make Mom more comfortable. It was so hard to endure sitting there, mostly by myself hour after hour. God would give me distractions that would make me smile. There was this little lady that was across the hall from my mom, and I would wave to her and send her kisses, and she would send them back to me.

Ecclesiastes 5:20 "They seldom reflect on the days of life, because God keeps them occupied with their gladness of heart." And, there was Alberta who would say, "I'm so ugly" and I could tell her how very pretty she was. Mom's roommate was somewhat anxious and would wander down the hall saying she needs her clothes. I could ease her mind by showing her clothes in her closet. I enjoyed these three ladies! I know they were there not only for me to help them, but to help me as I stayed with Mom. They made me smile!

Mom passed away quietly at 95 years of age. She was now pain-free and with Jesus, which gave me great relief because of His great care. I never thought when she came to live with my husband and I that she would live for eight more years. It was a tremendous blessing because God allowed her to be with her grandchildren, great-grandchildren, and she was able to meet two new great granddaughters that were born during her time with us. She would say, "Isn't family great! Even when my son, his wife and three children AND three dogs came to live with us for six months, I thought it would stress her out, but, it didn't. She'd sit and smile

169

and enjoy the love in the room. They all loved Max, and she loved them!

Any snippets of wisdom that I have to offer would be to realize that there will be challenges when caring for a loved one. The worst part for me is her mind not accepting my advice as it pertains to the care that she needed. There were times I was impatient with her because it concerned me when she wouldn't listen to me and not do things that would help her to feel better. It was as if she was sabotaging herself. I could only stand by and watch her health decline. When I had those moments, I would pray to God to help me and give me words of wisdom. I could watch God's fancy footwork the whole time. It makes me think of Psalm 8:4 "What is mankind that you are mindful of them, that you care for them". The sweetness of The Father melts my heart. "He was there every step of the way. He never forsook me or left me" Psalms 9:10. I thank God for the experience of caring for my mother. I'd do it all over again, a million times more, and love that she would be with me.

I feel so good knowing that I had her close and under my care. When your loved one is near, you can see them and hear them, so if there's ever a problem, you can correct it right away, and help to make their life better. It would've been so hard if Mom were in a nursing home far away from me. Or, if she had lived alone, I doubt that she would've lived as long as she did. I'm convinced that God used me and my abilities to care for her. I'm reminded of a verse in Isaiah 50:2, "Do I lack the strength to rescue you? By a mere rebuke I dry up the sea." God has done so much! It's difficult to parent your own parent and do the role reversal, but I'd do it all again if I could! Those were special times for my family and for me! I will always treasure those last years that my family and I had her with us. I'm so thankful for my husband's love and support with mom live. God did many big and small things during those eight years. In James 1:17 it says, "Every good and perfect gift is from above". When I see a good God helping me, I thank Him and He shows me more. I know and anticipate how He's going to work in my life. He wants to work in your life too! Come and experience what an awesome God He is!

Chapter 21

A Sense of Belonging

I was 16 and pregnant and didn't know where to turn. I had lived with the same foster family since I was six weeks old. When they found out I was pregnant they gave me an ultimatum; I could have the baby and leave, or I could have an abortion and stay. I didn't know of any place to go if kept the baby. So, scared of being alone, and not being a part of a family, I chose to have the abortion. It wasn't about right or wrong for me back then; it was about not wanting to be alone and not belonging.

After it was over my foster family acted as if it had never happened. Even though the rest of the family may have forgot about the abortion, I sure didn't! I felt so terrible about myself and began drinking more, doing drugs and having sex to escape the guilt. I thought I was the worse person in the world. Morally, I knew it was wrong to take a life. Over the next few years, I got pregnant and had several miscarriages. I believed God was punishing me for having an abortion. And, I thought I deserved it for taking an innocent life.

I'm not proud of it, but I lived an immoral life! I met this new guy, ended up pregnant and had an ectopic pregnancy, (which means that the egg was growing in my fallopian tube). The doctor had to remove the baby along with the fallopian tube. He said that my other tube was so scarred that I'd probably never be able to have a baby. That was crushing news! Although, I was raised by my foster family since I was a baby they never adopted me. I will always be a foster kid, which equates in my mind as '*unwanted.* All of my life, I was looking to be loved. I wanted someone to love me for me, unconditionally. That was the constant thought going through my mind…will I ever be loved? If truth be told I longed for my own child to love and to love me in return. Then I'd have a family, and my baby and I would love and belong to one another. I wanted a baby to help fulfill this desire in my heart!

One day, my mom and I went into a fast food burger place to eat. As I was waiting for my order, I heard a voice in my head. I believe God spoke to me and said that the boy at the grill was going to give me a baby. I looked around to see if someone close by talking to me. I know it sounds crazy, but I seriously did hear it. And, when I looked at the guy at the grill I didn't even think he was that cute. So, I didn't see me having a baby with him! My mom decided to talk to the manager about giving me a job and I got an interview right then, and a job. Max, the grill guy and I got to know one another, and we had fun together. We moved in together when I found out that I was three months pregnant. I know it sounds crazy, but I really did hear a voice tell me that he was going to be the father of my child. I didn't think God forgave me or loved me in my sinfulness...at least not yet. It's amazing that even with my immoral living God was planning my future.

I was pregnant at 24 years of age. Could the doctors have been wrong about me being too scarred inside to have a baby? I was thinking this could be my only chance, so I immediately stopped smoking, drinking and doing drugs. I wanted to do everything right, so I could carry the baby to full term. When I was 4 months along, I started bleeding and I was scared of another miscarriage and didn't want to be heartbroken again. I wasn't a believer at that time, but I knew there was a God. I prayed and pleaded with Him to let me keep my baby. Surely, He wouldn't let me carry a child this long when I had some hope of a family. Please God let me keep my baby! I was so thankful when the doctor told me that I probably wasn't going to lose her. I caught a glimpse of feeling a little loved by God during my pregnancy. I didn't think God was forgiving me or loved me in my sinfulness. But, I appreciated so much the mercy He showed me by allowing me to have a baby.

My little Angel was born six weeks early as a healthy, beautiful baby girl. She was my miracle baby! I'm so thankful that God allowed me to have my Angel. I've never been able to have a baby since, so I know God was involved. I feel so blessed to have her! Unfortunately, after a couple of years, her Dad and I separated when he went back to his old girlfriend. He chose not to be very involved in her life, but he did help us out financially. But, it was hard on Angel not seeing her Dad and not feeling wanted by him. I could relate to those feelings. I indulged her as much as I was able and I gave her as much of my time as I could with working and going to school. She's been my world and my greatest joy!

My life changed when Angel and I were going to church regularly and I began studying the Bible. When I accepted Christ as my Lord and Savior and was baptized I didn't feel much different, but I took the decision I made very seriously. It was about a month later when I was at worship when I sensed the forgiveness of God and I bawled like a baby. It was a pivotal moment in my spiritual walk. I felt such love and acceptance from God and from my church family.

> *"Anyone who **belongs to Christ** has become a new person. The old life is gone; a new life has begun!"*
> 2 Corinthians 5:17 ESV

It's been difficult forgiving myself for the wild life that I led, and most especially for having an abortion. I have to live with the decision that I made. The guilt of it doesn't ever leave! Even after becoming a Christian and knowing that He took away all of my sins, I still carry sadness for having an abortion. I will always regret it! I'm so grateful that no matter how awful of a person that I was, God took my shame and loves me, anyway. He has erased my sins and forgiven me. That's huge! God accepts me as His child and has welcomed me into His family! Now, at 32 years of age, I finally belong to a big family!

Chapter 22

Inhale the Future, Exhale the Past

By Stephanie McLean

August 23, 2013, a day that brought so many thoughts, emotions, and feelings for me, and my family. There are days where I feel like it's been years since Scott's passing, and other days I feel like it just happened yesterday and it all replays in my head. Scott was a wonderful man, loving husband, father, uncle, brother, and son. Never in my life did I think he would have died by suicide. I have a sign hanging in our home now that reads, 'Every family has a story, welcome ours'. This is our story.

The week leading up to my husband's passing had signs that something was really wrong with him. Scott was in the Army Reserve, and had seen 5 deployments, 4 of which were overseas. Every time he came home from a deployment, he had changed. After his last deployment to Afghanistan, during the out-processing phase, he had to take a mental health test. When the results were mailed to him weeks later, it was suggested that he needed to seek treatment for PTSD, but it was up to him to seek it. Scott would always tell me "I'm no worse off than anyone else" and "I don't need to get treatment".

Scott had been to drill the weekend before he died. He called me while he was at drill, and was complaining that things were changing and he wasn't happy about it, and he didn't understand how or why they could just change their minds about things last minute. From the time he walked in the door Sunday night after drill, I could tell something was wrong. A trigger had been switched on, and it was not good.

I remember one day that week, he sent me a text at work saying he needed to talk to me. When I got home, he was on the back deck drinking a beer. I could tell something was wrong, and I was worried. Scott proceeded to tell me through tears he wanted to be deployed again. He wanted to go back into a war zone because he felt safe there, could be in control and have his weapon on him. Scott looked me in the eyes and said, "What kind of person wants to go back to that? I shouldn't want to go back there and leave you and Max, but I want to go". As I sat there listening and looking at him, I told him if that's what you want to do, then find a unit that is being deployed and go back, that Max and I would be here waiting when he came home. I remember feeling scared, lost, and helpless. At one point in our conversation, I looked at Scott and asked him if he was suicidal because of the way he was acting and things he was saying and he told me, "No". To this day I can still hear him telling me "No, I'm not suicidal. Why would you even ask me that"? Another thing I remember him saying to me was, "If he deployed again, he probably wouldn't come home alive". And yet, he wanted to be deployed? I didn't understand why staying home with Max and I wasn't fulfilling for him. I wasn't comforted at all!

The next day he asked if I could take him to talk to his buddy from his unit that lived close to us. I thought maybe after Scott talked to him, it might make a difference, and he would feel better about everything. When I got off work, we headed to his friends' house. I dropped him off so they could talk in private, and went to get some dinner. An hour later he called and said he was ready to be picked up. On our way home, I asked him if he felt better after talking with his friend, and he said, "Yes". Scott did seem a little more upbeat then he had all week, but I was stilled worried. After we got home, I put the baby to bed. I remember lying in bed next to Scott, and he was a nervous wreck. He was so on edge, but somehow I managed to get some sleep that night.

Friday morning, I got up and was getting ready for work. Scott had told me the night before he had gotten in touch with someone at the VA in St. Louis, and he was going there for an appointment to try and help him through all of this. I told Scott I would call in to work, so I could drive him and he kept repeating "I just need to do this by myself". I went ahead and went to work with this fear of something still not being right. My sister came to our house to pick up our son Maxwell who was 7 ½ months old at that time. When she left my house she came to me at work and said she didn't really think Scott was going to go to the VA, he was going to sit at home and play video games, or go back to bed. While she was picking Max up, she put in the car seat and buckled him in, went back to his room to get the diaper bag, and when she came out Scott had taken Max out of the car seat. Erin asked him what he was doing and he said "I just wanted to hold him one more time".

The whole morning at work was horrible. I had asked my office manager if I could leave because something wasn't right with Scott, and she told me she knew she shouldn't have come to work that day, so I just dropped it and stayed. I tried calling Scott and texting him with no answer. I couldn't wait 'til 11:30 a.m. so I could go home for lunch and see if he had really gone to St. Louis to the VA, or what was going on.

As I was driving home, and was turning onto the road before our subdivision, I could see Scott's truck was still in the driveway. Panic instantly struck me. I was so scared to go in my house because I just had a feeling in my gut something was terribly wrong. The garage door opened, I got out of the car and came into the house and was greeted by our dog. I called out Scott's name several times, looked in our bedroom to see if he was in there, and then I walked around the corner of the kitchen table and looked back into our back family room. There was Scott, sitting on the couch, a pistol in his hand, blood on his face, his feet were black, and there was dried blood everywhere. I screamed his name, and immediately dialed 911. I was screaming on the phone to the dispatcher, and the only thing I remember saying was my name when she asked me. I ran outside and was going to our neighbor's house, that just so happened to be an on duty police officer, when she came flying down the road to help me.

I called my sister, screaming to her to hurry up and get here. I was all alone, scared, feeling sick at my stomach at what I had just seen. Another police officer showed up and was trying to get me to calm down and I couldn't. My sister, mom and Max got there and a family friend pulled up right behind them. My mind was spinning; I didn't know what to do. I couldn't process what had just happened. Someone brought me Scott's phone, and I called his buddy that he had talked with the night before. He was shocked at the news I told him. Before I knew it all of our close friends were there to support me. Police officers were asking me questions, the coroner was asking about what funeral home to use. I couldn't even think, let alone make decisions.

In the days and weeks to come, somehow, someway I survived. The first two years after Scott's passing are pretty much a blur in my mind. So many things in my mind are just gone now. Months later, I eventually was able to go to the police department and read the three page letter he had left behind.

Scott and I had to do IVF to become pregnant. The first round of IVF we had two embryos put in. Maxwell was a twin, and we found out at 11 weeks, baby "B" didn't have a heart beat anymore. We also had one embryo that was viable enough to be frozen. After Scott's death, I continued to pay the yearly storage fee to keep that one embryo frozen.

In the fall of 2015, I got a letter in the mail stating storage fees would be due at the beginning of 2016, and did I want to continue paying. I thought and prayed for a long time about what to do with the embryo. After discussing it with my family, and a few close friends, I decided that I wanted to try and have the embryo thawed, and have another baby. I put it all into Gods hands, and knew that no matter what the outcome was, I would have no regrets. Several doctor's visits, lots of injections and medication, it was time for the office to unthaw my embryo. It was a 50/50 chance as to whether or not it would be viable. I patiently waited for my phone call from the office, and when I got it they gave me my time and day for my frozen embryo transfer.

Erin, my sister, went with me that day. She had been my rock throughout everything that had happened after Scott passed away. The transfer went smoothly, and now to wait for two weeks for my blood test to find out if it worked. February 16th, 2016 I went in for my blood test. After I had my blood drawn, Max and I went to lunch and out to play. When I got the call, I was scared, nervous, and excited. The nurse said my counts looked great, to come in next week for more blood work to make sure the numbers were increasing. I truly thought this baby was a girl, and was completely surprised at my gender reveal party to find out Max was getting a brother.

On October 17, 2016, my sweet baby, Thatcher Jeffrey (same middle name as his daddy) was born via C-section. I'm so thankful and happy that God blessed me with this baby. He is Max's biological brother, and mine and Scott's baby. Who knew that when we froze that embryo almost 4 years prior, this would be our story? I vaguely remember the day Scott and I signed all the paperwork when we did IVF, if something were to happen to one of us, what would happen to the frozen embryo. In my mind I can hear him say, "You can do what you want with it if I'm dead". Who knew I would have to make the decision without him. Even through all of the darkness, Thatcher has brought so much light, joy, and happiness into our family.

Both boys are miracles, and keep me alive and moving. I thank God every day for getting me through the worst time in my life, when I was in such a dark place, and didn't know how I was going to survive. We talk about Scott every day. Max and Thatcher both look and act just like him. I love how even though neither of the boys ever knew their Daddy, there is so much of him inside of them. There are times when I'm not sure if I should laugh or cry, but at the end of the day, I know God has some pretty amazing plans in the future for my little family.

Our Scars Of Hope

Chapter 23

My wound stories cover many years. It's not just one wound story that I have to share, but a succession of them that took me on a journey where I would experience....

A Season of Forgiveness

Anna Kay Schmidt

I'm certain you would agree with me that the anticipation of having a baby is exciting! You can hardly wait to hold that sweet baby in your arms that you've carried for nine months. Soon after, family members arrive at the hospital carrying flowers and gifts, and take pictures of the newest family member, and discuss who she looks like. Well, the circumstances of my birth were most likely not filled with the typical joy and happiness for my parents.

I found out when I was in my 30s, that my Dad drove my Mom to the hospital to deliver me, but he didn't come back to pick us up after I was born. My aunt came to pick us up and took us home. It should've been a happy time, but instead it was mingled with sadness and loneliness for my Mom. It was quite a surprise to learn this as an adult! I was the youngest of four children born to my parents, who divorced not long after I was born.

My Mom met my Dad when he was in the service and stationed in the Philippine Islands. He married her and she became pregnant with my oldest sister. She soon sailed to America alone on a boat. Try to picture a scared teenager leaving her family and everything she knew, to have a chance for a better life in a new and foreign land. I don't think I could have done it! My Mom is a first-generation immigrant and had been in the states about seven years when she gave birth to me. She didn't speak English very well, or even write or read it, or know much about our currency, and she

181

didn't drive either. I knew all of these things about my Mom before I learned about my Dad not picking my Mom and me up at the hospital. But, somehow imagining what that situation looked like for her made everything that my Mom went through to come to America, and all that she had to overcome without the man who brought her halfway around the world, raised my respect for my Mom a hundred fold. Divorce is hard enough by itself, then you add the fact that she's thousands of miles away from her family and mothering four children alone without the help from my Dad. It had to make life nearly unbearable for her! Her saving grace was that she lived next to my grandparents, and across the street from my aunt and uncle, and other in-laws were only minutes away to help her. In fact, it was one of my aunts that took my Mom to a dance where she met my Step-Dad.

He had to have been crazy in love to marry her with four children 10 years old and younger. I don't know too many men that would do that and not have their own children too. Growing up, it was obvious how much he loved and adored my Mom. And, he loved me and I loved and respected him and called him 'Dad'. He was a constant and predictable figure in my life. I can see it so much clearer now as an adult. He rescued my Mom and all four of us kids. I'm so thankful for him!

Now, let's fast forward several years...

Mountains & Valleys

What? Move to Colorado? Why? But we just built our dream home at the edge of the state park and we were going to live here forever, remember? But, the kids and I don't want to move. I know, you got a great job offer with a lot more money and prestige. Yes, I hear Colorado's beautiful too! OK, if you think it's best for the family, let's go!

It all looked good, but looks can be deceiving. My marriage looked like that too! I didn't realize it at the time, but I would see all too soon how the great 'deceiver' (Satan) works. Just when I thought life was going well for our family of five, Satan would make his 'checkmate' move!

We had a large beautiful new home in northern Colorado. My husband had a job where they appreciated him. We had more money to take weekend trips with our three children to visit local attractions. The schools were good! We had found a new church family that we liked. We all made new friends. All three of the kids were playing soccer, with the oldest two on club teams. We were spending more time together as a family enjoying recreational Colorado. Life was good!

A few months before the bottom of my world fell out, some ladies from church invited me to a weekly Bible study with them. I was excited to begin the study and desired to get to know God on a deeper level. Little did I know that I didn't need to attend the bible study for that lesson because my life was about to embark me on a journey that would rip at my innermost being. It would throw me into a battle that I was uncertain at times if I would survive, or if I even wanted to.

I found out several months after moving that one of my husband's favorite times of recreation in Colorado wasn't fly-fishing, but spending time with a woman at his work. I was angry and very hurt! The idea of him with another woman devastated me! How do I handle this? This is so foreign to me. I remember hearing and reading about adultery in the Bible and wondered why God mentioned it so many times in the Bible. It's even one of the 10 commandments listed in Exodus 20. After the initial shock somewhat wore off, my husband, and I talked and decided that we were going to work through it and keep our marriage and family together. Naturally, he vowed to give her up, and he did, time and time again. Promises were made and broken many times. To say that life was tough then was an understatement!

We didn't tell our children that we were having problems (as if they couldn't hear the yelling and me crying hysterically), and we most definitely, did not tell our parents right away. I didn't want mine to know, so they wouldn't hold it against him when we got through all of it. I was trying to be positive about some things. Or, so I thought. But really, it was keeping Satan happy that my husband, and I didn't seek help. And, in the meantime he had 'her' to talk to.

I felt alone. My depression deepened. I tried to get his attention by choosing to go for night walks around the neighborhood or on drives where I'd park for an hour or two to try to rationalize what was happening to our family. Sometimes I'd walk to the subdivision across the street that was under construction and lie down on the plywood floors and talk and cry out to God in the dark. Most of the time, I felt like God wasn't listening, because my marriage wasn't better. And, I wasn't better either. I was feeling defeated. My husband didn't seem to care when I would venture off at night. To my disappointment, he would be fast asleep when I got home. He just solidified how invaluable I felt.

A couple of times I drove up to the mountains ready to drive right off a cliff. He told me I wasn't a good wife or mother, and I believed him. So what did it matter if I lived? Apparently, I had treated those I loved the most, the worst, according to him. Once, I had even written my final letter to him and left it at the house before I drove off. I didn't care about myself anymore. I was in such a dark place. I would cry the 30 minutes it took me to get up in the mountains. I would look for a good spot that would end it for me, and not leave me a cripple, and a burden to my family. But, in that moment, the good Lord whispered to me, "They need you! Your children need their Mom!" Something clicked inside, and I would think that's right, they do need me! I would break down and cry and thank God for saving me! He had just given me the bit of energy I needed to keep pressing forward. I had hit this place a few times, but each time God brought me back.

I needed someone to talk to who might understand. The longer his affair continued, the more people knew of it. I was embarrassed and felt like I was being judged. What reason did I give for him to look for someone else? Why wasn't he happy with me as his wife? Satan is crafty and devious and filled my head with lies! I know that God is omnipotent 'all powerful', omnipresent 'all-present' and, omniscient 'all-knowing'. I had realized that Satan could listen to my prayers and deceive me, but if I said my prayers in my head, only God could hear and know them. It was at this time when I stopped saying my prayers out loud. I had to have a spiritual battle plan and Satan not hearing my prayers gave him a disadvantage in my mind. It made perfect sense to me. I needed people to vent to, and to offer sound advice, because I wasn't thinking clearly. Satan wanted me to be alone, so he could tell me lies. Eventually, we decided to go to counseling appointments together and separately. I'd like to say it brought us back together and our marriage was saved, but continuing sin kept us disconnected.

I wanted him to feel guilty for what he did and to promise me that he'd never do it again. After all, he was a Christian man and was supposed to know better. There were many conversations, threats, pleadings, counseling sessions, tears, glasses flying and breaking, midnight rides alone, hikes in the mountains, and talks with friends to try to find some sanity. I prayed and asked others to pray and yet it didn't get better. I kept wondering where God was in the midst of the mess! Why wasn't He changing him? I expected him to jump through hoops to 'win' me over. He should appreciate me for staying with him, and not moving the kids back to our home in the south. Well, you can guess how well that worked! I felt rejected, unwanted, and undesired! I was extremely hurt! What was wrong with me? How could he do this to me and the kids? I didn't work outside the home, because we had agreed that I would stay at home when we had children. Our first child arrived 17 months after we were married. I had quit college after 2 ½ years because he said, "I didn't need a degree to stay at home and he would always support me". So, here I was without a degree and with three children. I wondered what I was going to do to help support myself. I had been totally dependent on him during our marriage. I thought of going back to school, but I wasn't in the mindset to make a decision about a career. It was time for me to go back to work.

I was trying to handle everything as best as I could. I prayed for God to be the Pilot in my circumstances, and I would be the co-pilot. Months later it was revealed to me that God doesn't need me to help Him steer. I needed to give all my problems to Him and let Him completely have control to guide me down this path. I gave it to God, but I kept taking it back out of His hands. I still hadn't learned that I was the one getting in the way of God's healing for me. I don't even know how I thought I could make good decisions since I was such an emotional mess.

When you're in the pit of despair, with fear as your motivator, you don't make good decisions. My life was a testament to that truth. Satan was grinning with how I was behaving. I wasn't giving my husband a reason to want to stay with me with the way I was acting. I didn't realize that at the time because I was reacting to the situation, and not honestly seeing 'why' he did what he did. I was too deeply wounded to see his point of view. It didn't occur to me that he was wounded too! "I do not understand what I do. For what I want to do, I do not do." Romans 7:25

He moved out after thirteen months of his 'revelation to me' and we were divorced nine months later. When it came time to sign the divorce papers, I sobbed in the courtroom. I had never felt such hurt and rejection in my life, especially from someone who had made a covenant with me and with God to love me forever. I guess it was easy for him since he said, "he'd never really loved me for nearly 17 years". Seriously!

I was so wounded and tried to pick up the pieces. I was surviving because of my children. I had no other reason to go on. Daily, I managed to get the kids to and from school and to soccer practices. I somehow managed to coach my 5-year-olds soccer team. I guess it gave me something to feel good about since the team was good. Many days, I went back to bed because I was depressed. Maybe if I went to sleep, I would wake up and it would all be a nightmare. I had some very dear friends that would ring my doorbell until I answered it and insist I get dressed, so they could take me to lunch. They were persistent! I may not have acted grateful to them at the time, but they were my lifesavers! God was working, because he sent them to help me during a very dark time in my life. I'm forever indebted to them for their love and friendship.

I had just experienced the death of my marriage. What do I do now? This death wasn't instantaneous as in an accident, but slow over many years. When my eyes were puffy from crying and my insides felt ripped apart, all I could think about was finding some bandages to stop the bleeding. My head couldn't wrap around this much hurt. What could I have possibly done to contribute to it?

There were years where I felt insignificant in my husbands' eyes. I tried to do things to gain his approval. I thought taking care of my appearance, being Suzy homemaker, PTO leader, Bible class teacher, a loving mother, soccer coach and attentive wife was good enough. All of those things are well and good, but unkind words spoken over time can cause us to react ungraciously towards one another. When I told him how I felt, he would tell me not to feel that way. I wanted him to be proud of me. It seems when a standard was set, then met, the bar was raised and I had to try again. I believe over time, I got tired of trying to perform to win his love and acceptance. I would shut down at times, and I'm sure it showed in my actions, or should I say the lack of them. I imagine he saw it and felt it and he concluded that I didn't care. We were a couple looking for love and acceptance from one another, each waiting for the other to give it first. I believe we each did nice things, but if not reciprocated, then it stopped. He told me after our divorce that he knew just how far to push me, then he would be nice and bring me back around, so I would feel better.

We should've had counseling years ago, but it had a negative connotation back in the 80s & early 90s, so it wasn't even a momentary thought for us. We weren't that messed up that we needed counseling! It was another one of Satan's lies, because we really did need it! We just didn't think we did. The journals I kept echoed my loneliness and feelings of depression. Divorce doesn't typically happen in a short amount of time. It's a build-up of unmet expectations and words said that you can't take back and even some you can never forget. Our marriage faded away slowly over the years and we hadn't even noticed it happening. I mentioned earlier about Satan being crafty and devious. I hadn't noticed he had been working a long time to slowly destroy our marriage.

I tried to move forward now that I was single, so a friend set me up on a date with a co-worker. He was nice! And, I really liked the attention he gave me. We got along well and had fun together. I really was still a mess inside, but he made me feel wanted and desirable. But, that would turn out to be a bad thing. He was separated from his wife, because she had a boyfriend. The reality was he was still married, but I conveniently pushed that aside in my mind. I found out all too soon, just how easy it is to be lured into the temptation of adultery. I ended the relationship when I realized it was too soon for me to date, and it was especially way

187

too soon for my children. When my ex-husband found out that I had dated someone, I think he got a little jealous and he suggested we try dating again. Deep inside, I was still bleeding from our divorce. I desperately wanted our family back together. I thought maybe he'd hit his bottom and was ready to work on us now. I was still so wounded and now I'd added the guilt of my own bad choices to the mix. Oh, and my 'ex' reminded me of my wrongs. It was easy to turn the tables and put the focus on me, instead of him. Yup! We're still messed up! I too, found it easier to look at his mistakes, and not see how I could be better. We dated off and on for about a year after our divorce. I got a lot of empty promises! He would stop seeing her, but it was only a couple of weeks before he boomeranged back to her. I finally wised up after going to a psychiatrist who helped me to see the emotional and mental abuse that this was doing to me. I realized and accepted that he really didn't want me. He just didn't want anyone else to have me. I finally decided to end the emotional rollercoaster and move forward. It was a tough decision, but it was the right one. *"Heal me Oh Lord and I will be healed."* Jeremiah 17:14a (NIV)

In the midst of all the marriage/divorce drama, our daughter was making bad choices and lying to us about where she went and what she did. My motherly instincts kicked in, but at the time it was easier to live in denial. I just pushed it back in the deep recesses of my mind as if whatever she had been doing wasn't happening. If you don't think it's real, then you don't have to deal with it, right?

My middle child wasn't doing well in school. He was quiet when it came to talking about his feelings. That's common for a 6th grader, right? He loved playing soccer and riding bikes with his friend in the neighborhood. He was good to play with his younger brother who was in 1st grade. I spent a lot of time with the kids after the divorce and tried to make up for our family being broken. It's not possible to fix it, but I tried the best I knew how in the moment. I loved them and wanted them to feel secure in my love. I hope I was successful! I think I was.

I wondered if God heard my prayers. Someone had told me to talk to God like a friend. I remember crying and yelling out to God because I felt so burdened, "Can you please pick on someone else?

188

I have enough going on! I don't need this!" Well, this was me being open and honest with God. I wanted the constant pain inside to stop! I asked people not to pray that I have strength. Because to be stronger, only meant in my mind that I would get more pain to handle. Oh and add 'patience' to that request...don't pray for me to have patience either. I was at my wit's end already and did not need more hurt, pain or time. I was overwhelmed and tired! Sometimes when I was driving, I was so deep in thought that when I arrived at my destination, I couldn't even recall anything about my drive. "How did I get here?" My brain was in a fog! I wasn't thinking clearly. I was a mess!

When I looked in the mirror, I saw someone who was angry, hurt, embarrassed and disappointed with my life. I moved in closer and I noticed the scar across the bridge of my nose and between my eyebrows. When did that happen? These scars will always be a reminder of the many tears and the extreme sadness of the realization that my marriage was over, and our family was broken forever.

Looking For the Light

"How could this be happening to MY family? This isn't the way it's supposed to be! I feel so scared. Why can't they understand me?! I can't believe my parents LIED to me! How could they do this to me...and my brothers? Why aren't they doing more? Why is this happening? I'm so tired of feeling misunderstood. What is my life going to look like now? I'm so tired of feeling sad and alone. I'm not sure I even care if I live or die anymore."

These were the thoughts of my heartbroken daughter when she was 14 years old. Too young to have fully formed emotionally to be able to gather up any peace of mind of what has happened. Unable to put into words that the family she's known and trusted had completely changed. Her world, and all of ours, had flipped upside down.

As a parent, you want to do ANYTHING in the world to protect, love, and make sure your child never feels anything like this. What do you do when you know your child is broken and don't know how to help? What do you do as a parent when you're broken too? What do you do when the light at the end of the tunnel begins to fade and you're stumbling in the darkness?

This was the reality of my life and that of my daughter in 1998. As a mother, I had hopes and dreams for Aimee. I encouraged her and was happy to help her be all that she could be in this world and for eternity. I wanted her to have new experiences, her own opinions and be alright with sharing them and doing what was right in God's eyes.

She was an obedient child and did as she was told. She was caring, thoughtful, and did very well in school, played piano and was an outstanding soccer player. I was very proud of my firstborn child and only daughter!

When she was 8 years old, she was the only girl that played on the boys' travel soccer team. She learned to be tough and held her own as she played with the boys. As a freshman in high school she played on the Varsity team. It was so enjoyable to watch her on the field. She played with such passion!

Aimee began changing and chose a different road than the one that we had planned for her, and that she had laid out for herself when she was 14. One of her high school teachers called me to tell me that she had noticed her grades were declining. She also told me she had written a paper about marijuana and how it should be legalized. She feared she was smoking pot. Great! Just what I didn't need to hear about my sweet daughter. I was saddened and surprised by her phone call. I found it odd that a teacher would take the time to call a parent and share their concern for their student in this manner. Something was going on and I feared what I might find out. Maybe I'd rather live in denial, then know the truth.

There were a few times that I had caught her smoking a cigarette on the front porch swing. She denied smoking when I asked her about it. "Really, I see the cigarette butt in the grass that you just threw over there when I came out the door." It was one of the many lies to come. It was obvious that she had grown apathetic. It was so sad to see her like this because it was so out of character for her. She was usually so fun loving and spunky!

I remember a time she came home from shopping with inappropriate clothing for a 9th grader that she had bought at the mall. I told her to return them because she wasn't allowed to wear them. She became angry with me and told me that she liked them and she wasn't returning them! I'd not seen this side of her before. Who was this child anyway?

Her brothers didn't want to be around her, because she was negative and snarky, and just not fun anymore. They all had been close once and enjoyed one another, but it sure wasn't like this lately. It hurt my heart to watch all of this going on between my three children. There were so many things going on inside my head. I didn't know where to start or what to do!

At the time, it had been a couple of years since the earthquake of their dad's affair. We stayed together for a year, arguing a lot, hoping the kids wouldn't hear, but unfortunately, they did. We eventually separated and divorced a few weeks before our 17th wedding anniversary.

How does this happen to a Christian family that goes to church three times a week, reads Bible bedtime stories to their kids and who promises their children that they would never get divorced like their school friends' parents? I'm pretty sure that my kids were feeling some of the same feelings that I had as little by little our seemingly 'perfect' world was destroyed. Where was the trust and honesty and especially, the faith that we preached to them? I imagine in our children's eyes their parents looked like hypocrites and liars. Everything that they'd been taught in their life was now in shambles and destroyed, just as a tornado can so quickly demolish a house, so was our family. So, what and why should they believe now? How do they rebuild their lives after the devastation? And, how do I help them pick up the pieces of what's left?

I was depressed and angry at what the divorce did to our family, and especially to my kids! I was so wounded myself, I found it difficult to know what to do to help my three children cope after everything we'd known as a family was tossed away. Aimee desperately needed me and was trying to get my attention by acting out. I knew something wasn't right with her. I tried to talk to her, but she would just tell me what I wanted to hear. She was such a sad girl! Her 'boo-boo' was just too big to kiss and make it all better this time! Help!

She continued down her road of self-destruction. One night in July, she snuck out of the house to go to a Pink Floyd concert, after she was told she couldn't attend, because of her negative behavior. Well, Aimee was going to do what Aimee wanted to do. She had left a note on her bed that said,

> *"I'm very sorry + I love you guys, but I'm going to Pink Floyd. I've been waiting for many months. I am very sorry and I'll be back tomorrow. I love you."* Aimee ♡

I didn't know what to do because I was surprised that she had left. I decided to call her Dad. I thought maybe we could figure something out together. Two heads are better than one, right? Maybe in a different situation. Or, with two different people. It was easy for us to blame each other for the fact that she snuck out and went to the concert.

We knew we had to wait until she would come back into town after the concert. We called around to some of her friends' houses and eventually were told that some of the kids were staying at one of the boys' house nearby.

It was after midnight, but we knew where he lived, so we drove over there. We rang the doorbell, but no one answered. Then we saw kids darting back and forth in the house, so we knew someone was home. Why wouldn't they open the door? It was getting so frustrating!

Out of desperation, her dad called the police. A policeman showed up and he knocked on the door and called out through the door for someone to come out. But, no one did. Scenes like this were not a normal occurrence in our lives. Several months ago, Aimee was a dot your 'I's and cross your T's kind of gal. This kind of behavior from her was so foreign to us. The policeman told us, "No law was being broken. She was willingly in the house, and didn't want to come out, and there wasn't anything he could legally do about it." This was not the news that I wanted to hear! "You're not serious, right? Make her come out!" played in my head. I wanted to get our daughter out of that house and take her home! But, NO, we had to leave and wait until morning to hopefully, hear from her. I felt utterly helpless and hopeless! In my mind I had just won the terrible parent award! What had happened to our family? How did we get here?

It was a long night of crying and calling out to God for help. I often wondered if He grew tired of hearing me whine. The past couple of years were very difficult. At times, I even wanted to throw in the towel, because the hurt was so intense. Waiting on God to turn things around is so very hard to do. And, it's especially hard when it involves your teenage child. Eventually, she did call me for a ride home the next morning, after being coerced by her friend's mom. I think I jumped into the car quicker than I ever had before to bring Aimee home. I knew that I had to be careful with my words. I couldn't react in anger because she was already so fragile. I was upset with her, but, oh, how I loved her! I also knew she had to be hurting so much, to be so disobedient by sneaking out of the house. What had happened to my innocent daughter?

There was so much despair and darkness that it was hard to see where to take the next step. Which way led to the light? I knew that I'd been leaning more on my own human wisdom and strength than on Gods. It was obvious that I was in way over my head, and making a mess, I might add. Life was spiraling out of control. Aimee was so hurt and lost, and her Dad and I just weren't handling things well. Psalms 55:2 says, *"Please listen and answer me, for I am overwhelmed by my troubles."* I prayed earnestly that God would help her and give her new friends to help her find her way. This was the start of me learning to give God control <u>again</u>. Aimee and I were both a mess! We needed God to show His power in our lives.

It was September 13, 2000 when Aimee told me that she had gone with her girlfriend to a meeting that helps teenagers with drug problems. She said that the counselor had asked her to bring her parents with her to the next meeting! Ohhh-Kaaay! It's ironic, because instead of us begging her to go for help, she's asking her Dad and me to go. Immediately we jumped on board in hopes this was going to work for her.

I was scared to go to the meeting. It was now confirmed that Aimee had a drug problem, and she knew it! And now, I knew she had a serious enough problem that she needed help. It's tough facing the sad truth, but, I'm thankful that she saw it and was seeking help.

It was time for the parent meeting. Her Dad and I walked in united on Aimee's behalf. You can imagine my surprise when we walked in and I saw people that I knew. Thoughts ran through my head, 'Oh, so it was your son, or your daughter who did drugs with Aimee'. Sadly enough, having all of us there was eye opening and yet, comforting. I wasn't alone in this battle. Now, I could talk with someone who understood the pain of having a child being a drug user and not feel judged. The Lord knows I've had more than my share of loneliness lately.

That night, her Dad and I agreed to enroll her into the teenage drug rehabilitation program. It would be an intensive 12 week outpatient program. She would be there every day working the program. It was a sad reality! But, I was thankful for this answer to my prayer.

When I drove Aimee there the next day, she begged me not to make her go inside. "I don't feel comfortable with them. They're not like me! Did you not see their face piercings, purple and pink hair and tattoos? We're too different! Please Mom don't make me go!" I reminded her that two of her friends were there and she had drugs in common with all of them. I promised to be back to pick her up. She reluctantly went inside. My heart was hurting and tears were flowing! This was the beginning of a new road for her. It would be up to her to pave the way.

One night when I was going to pick her up, it occurred to me that God had answered my prayers, because she now had *new friends to help her,* just as I had prayed. It was like a light had been turned on in my head. When I realized this answer to my prayer, I began crying and thanking Him as I drove down Wilson Avenue. It wasn't the way I would've chosen to help her. And, I certainly didn't have a teenage drug rehab program in mind. But, *"His ways are not our ways".* Isaiah 55:8

The counselor mentioned that it was months of being in the program before Aimee even started smiling. She said, "She looked dead inside". She wasn't working the program, so it was time to go to the next step. Boy, she was good at fooling me, because I thought she was doing well. It was suggested that she move to Denver to live with a family whose daughter had a year of sobriety and was in the teen program. This crushed my heart! Aimee was very upset about moving! Her dad and I weren't happy with it either, but we wanted our daughter to be drug free. If she had to move out at age 16, then so be it! It was very difficult for all of us! Never in a million years did I ever think my sweet, little, precious Aimee would have a drug and alcohol problem and we would have to encourage her to move in with complete strangers. We were able to take her to the house and meet the parents and the family. It was with them and her being in Denver that she finally started working the program.

I attended the weekly parent meetings in Denver, and I also was able to visit with Aimee. I wanted her to know that even at her lowest, and most difficult and darkest times, I loved her and was there for her. Eventually, I could see that she was getting back to her ole' sweet self. I discovered that I needed to attend those meetings for my own healing. There's a newsflash! God was of course, working on me too!

Since she moved, she also had to leave her high school and be home-schooled with the group. She graduated early and grew up fast...too fast! She gave up a lot with her choice to drink and do drugs. A soccer scholarship to college was now a dream of the past. There are consequences to the choices that we make in life.

Through all of this I couldn't help wondering what kind of parent people thought I was if they had known that my teenage daughter had a drug problem. Often, I wanted to run and hide and not deal with people's judgments! I felt like I'd already had their eyes embedded in the back of my head the past two years, and now, there was Aimee to talk about. The despair of it all was overshadowed by her working the program and becoming drug free. So overall, it was worth it! We had experienced the light of hope!

Looking back, I saw that I was concerned with how my life looked to people. It wasn't all wrapped up in a nice pretty bow! Oh, far from it! My box was crushed and the giftwrap was ripped and the bow was frayed. But, you know what? There was still a surprise in the box...the gift was inside. It's such a fallacy today to think no one has problems or skeletons in their closets. We live in a fallen world after all, and we're all sinners. But, Jesus died on the cross for **all** of us and He can wipe away all of our sins away, if we choose to obey and follow Him.

We went through much hurt and sadness to get to a better destination. The alternative would've been so much more horrific! Aimee told me she would've been dead had she not entered the 3-year program. She said the program saved her life! A number of her friends couldn't quit doing drugs. Unfortunately, even at her young age, she's gone to many of her friends' funerals that had overdosed. It's too real and heartbreaking!

We all make choices in life and we have to deal with the consequences whether they're good or bad. Aimee made choices based on her parent's decision to divorce. She decided to use alcohol and drugs to numb the extreme pain that she couldn't handle. She thought they were her answer, but it only took her further downward into a deeper, darker pit. The choices and decisions we make have a ripple effect that can either help or hurt others. Satan does a good job of discouraging us and deceiving us! He wants us to believe his lies. But, with God on our side we win! We're OVERCOMERS! **What a gift!**

Aimee graduated after three years of working the drug rehab program. I was so proud of her! She's had the opportunities to use her bad and negative choices to share with middle school students about the dangers of drugs and alcohol. I was happy that she wanted to help others kids. We also paid it forward by having a teenage girl from out East live in our home for a while as she learned to become drug free.

I learned a lot walking with Aimee on her drug free journey too! Just because a kid has body piercings, tattoos, or purple, blue, or green hair doesn't mean there's something wrong with him. I think they've simply found something they can have control over in their life, because too many things are chosen for them by their parents. I know the kids from the program that visited in my home were kind and respectful people and I grew to care about each one of them. I've learned *not* to judge a book by its cover, because it's what's inside that matters most.

I've also learned that those days were some of the darkest that I've ever gone through. It's hard to watch your child struggle with something that you know nothing about. But, I was able to see God at work and He made a better person out of me through the process. I've learned that if you want to get out of the darkness, it's best to let God's light lead the way.

Psalms 41:10 *"Don't be afraid, for I am with you. Don't be dismayed, for I am your God. I will strengthen you. I will help you. I will uphold you with my victorious right hand."* You don't have to go through your struggles alone. Give Him a call…. He's waiting to help.

Letting Go

It seems over the past few years that I was learning to accept loss in my life in different ways. I had the death of my marriage which meant the loss of my goal of ever making it to a 50th wedding anniversary as my ex in-laws families had achieved. Divorce of my marriage also developed into the loss of our family unit. None of us would ever be the same. In the middle of all the divorce drama, I had also lost my purebred 8-month-old dog that I was going to breed, when in its excitement to see my son it ran out into the road and was struck by a car and instantly killed the day before my birthday. Then, my daughter's choice to use drugs brought about the loss of dreams in her life, and the aspirations that I had for her as well. I had different avenues of 'letting go' to deal with in my life over a period of a few years. And, little did I know that there were more around the next bend. One of my favorite verses during those dark days was *"Heal me Lord and I will be healed"*. Jeremiah 17:14a I even had it inscribed in Hebrew in a necklace for me to wear and remember this promise often.

At the beginning of my Season of Forgiveness chapter I mentioned my Step Dad. He had been in my life since I was a baby. He wasn't my biological dad, but in all other aspects, he was my dad. He cared for me, raised me, disciplined and loved me. He will always remain a very important father figure in my life. I'm very thankful for him and what he taught me.

He was a big, strong construction worker. He was stern when he had to be, yet loving and unselfish. He was always thinking of others, especially of my Mom first of course, who he loved and adored. He helped many with handyman tasks. I thought he could do just about anything. He was a compassionate man, not only towards people, but towards animals. He rescued his dog, Patch a Staffordshire terrier when he was working in a house and noticed the neighbor kept him on a chain with no dog house in the back of the yard. He was skinny and barely got enough to eat. My Dad would give him his sandwich and water to drink from his lunchbox. He asked the neighbor if he could buy the dog and was told, "NO"! He continued to bring food for Patch each day he worked there over the next couple of weeks. One day, after noticing his chain was unable to reach his water bowl, and that he had to sit out in the rainstorm, he went back and told the neighbor that he was going to call the authorities with how horrible he was treating the dog. He gave the man his phone number and said that he would pay him for the dog and to give him a call. My Mom happened to answer the phone when the call came. The man said, "Tell him I've decided to sell the dog. He can come pick him up." My mom wasn't happy about getting a dog, but she understood that he wasn't cared for by his owner. She agreed for Patch to come to the house as long as he stayed outside. My dad hurried out the door to pick him up. Well, Patch won my mom over in no time and he was allowed to come inside the house. She grew a soft spot for him too! But, I've never seen a dog love a person more than Patch, also called Bud, loved my Dad. It's like Bud knew he had been rescued and he was going to be the best dog to show his gratitude. He was always going on jobs with him in his truck. Sometimes my Dad would treat him to a cheeseburger at McDonald's. He spoiled him with treats, but mostly with love. It was apparent to everyone how much they loved one another. I remember my Dad telling me "You can tell a lot about a person by the way they treat animals". You know he was right because he showed much love by his actions.

It was August 2001 when I was told that he had esophageal cancer. He had smoked for about 20 years, but had quit more than 30 years ago. I guess he couldn't undo the damage he had caused in his earlier years when cigarettes had no filters. He started chemotherapy and he did pretty well. He was a fighter. He still managed to do odd jobs for people especially those who were in hard times and couldn't pay. He had such a caring heart. Even during his illness, he was thinking about others. I remember how he also loved to make waffles every Saturday morning. When I'd be visiting, friends and family that lived close by would stop by to join him and my Mom for breakfast. Their kitchen table was filled with love and friendship.

He may have thought he was fooling everybody with his activity, but his tests showed something else. He began having trouble breathing and swallowing and in December he had exploratory surgery. The news wasn't good! The cancer had spread to his lungs and his liver. He would have radiation and chemotherapy. I flew back a couple months later and sat with him during one of his 4-5 hour chemotherapy treatments. It was nice to meet the doctor and medical staff that had been caring for him. I was beginning to understand cancer more than I wanted. My children wanted to see Grandpa over their Easter break, so we made the 17 hour drive to visit him. They loved him very much! It was difficult for them to see how much weight he had lost. They remembered a large burly man. My kids and I had been through so much the past few years. This was another heartache for all of us.

When I was at home in Colorado, I'd talk to my sister and brother that lived close to my parents to get updates on his condition. I didn't want to ask my Mom too many questions and possibly upset her. It had to be so hard watching the cancer slowly wither away the man that she adored and loved. When I came back in September, he had lost a total of 80 pounds. He was so thin and frail looking. I hope my reaction to seeing him didn't startle him. I mostly hurt inside my heart for him. If he was scared, he didn't show it. I think he thought he could beat cancer. He was so brave.

He went to Thanksgiving at my sister-and-brother-in-law's house that year and had a lot of difficulty using the stairs. He had been so positive going through his treatments. When he had trouble walking down the stairs he said, "I don't know what happened. I thought everything was going so well". It was eye opening to him. There was this realization in his eyes that he wasn't going to get better. It was sad! He had fought so hard the past year.

It wasn't long before hospice came to the house. A hospital bed was set up in the living room. The last couple of days my sister, who's a nurse stayed at their house to help turn him every two hours, so the fluid wouldn't fill his lungs. I knew that he didn't have much longer to live. I called him on December 26 in the evening and talked to him and told him that I wanted to sing him one of the songs that he always sang to me. "You are my sunshine, my only sunshine, you make me happy when skies are gray..." I sang the song and told him how much he meant to me and that I loved him. He said, "I love you too"! Early the next morning when my sister turned him over, he coughed and he took his last breath. Little did I know that me singing to him the night before would be the last time I'd ever sing for him. I'm so happy that I called him when I did. The timing was perfect! God knew it. I have peace in my heart that he died knowing he'd made a difference in my life and that I loved him.

I've wondered what Bud thought happened to his Master, who never returned when he was wheeled out the door. It's really sad to think about. To show just how special Bud was to him, an 8x10 picture of Bud sat on top of my Dad's casket during his funeral services. I wasn't jealous. Oh, if we all only loved with that kind of loyalty the world would be a better place.

Losing him was very hard! I still needed him around with everything that I had going on in my life. His love and care for me was constant and was probably the closest I've experienced as truly unconditional. I wanted him to teach my boys about carpentry. There have been many times that I've remembered him bringing me with him as he did odd jobs for people when I was a little girl. He'd give me some pieces of wood, a hammer and some nails and let me make something. Maybe that's one of the reasons that I've been good at crafts myself. Other times, when he was helping to build a new house I'd search every room for the electric box 'nickels' that I'd find on the floor thinking I'd found treasures. Sometimes, when we drove out in the country, we'd stop along the road in late spring and cut some wild asparagus. I have such wonderful memories of him and the time that we've spent together. I hate that cancer took him away too soon!

It was my Dad that first took me to church when I was a child. Many times we'd watch Billy Graham on TV together while Mom was working. I'm so thankful that he didn't give up on meeting my Mom at the dance hall when he decided to come one last time to see if she was there. God not only provided her a wonderful loving husband, but He helped me later in life to realize that someone doesn't have to be blood to love and care for you as if you were. I'm so very thankful for God's provisions! His blood didn't run through my veins, but I will remember him as my Dad who showed me and others what love looked like. He was one of my greatest blessings! What a legacy he left!

Mixed Blessing

Nearly six months after my Dad passed away, I met a man on an online Christian dating service, who after getting to know him better, turned out to be a lot like my Dad. This new guy seemed to be everything and more than I wanted! I was floating on cloud nine! The past four years had brought so much sadness and loss that I expected more of the same. Even though every day wasn't bad, this season of happiness was welcoming! We would become engaged and after we married, I decided to move to the Midwest where he was born, raised, lived and worked. Although, Colorado was a beautiful place to live, it also holds the deepest sadness for me. So, I was fine with moving away and starting over. This decision would produce an outcome I never saw coming.

I told my ex-husband I was engaged and planned to move several months later after school was out with our youngest child who was in 6th grade at the time. He quickly married the next month and told his family and me about it afterwards.

When my Ex and I divorced four years earlier, I was given residential custody of our three children. My oldest daughter was now living on her own and working. My second child was going to be graduating from high school in a few months and planned to go away to a technical school in the fall. Therefore, it was natural for me to assume my youngest would be moving with me. He made friends easily, was a decent soccer player and made good grades. So, adjustment to a new school in a new home town should be fairly easy for him. My oldest two did fine making new friends when we moved to Colorado. Naturally, I assumed he would do well too! It all made perfect sense to me.

There's six years age difference between my youngest and his middle brother. I felt bad that he was only in kindergarten when his Dad and I started fighting. He doesn't have much recollection of us all being a family. The thought of that makes me sad. We spent a lot of one-on-one time together while his sister and brother were in school. I had coached his recreational league soccer team since he was 4 years old during the spring and fall seasons, until he played on a club team when he was 10 years old. I attended his school events and helped out when I could. We sang songs together in the car, read stories and prayed together each night at bedtime.

I was busy making wedding and moving plans, only to find out that my Ex was going to fight me for custody. WHAT?!! I have to admit that I had some unchristian thoughts running through my head. It was now obvious to me that I needed to start preparing for the battle of our child. I noticed with his quick wedding and the big new house that his plan had already begun. A child advocate was assigned to our son by the court system. She met with him in each of our homes. He willingly sat on my lap at the kitchen table as she questioned me and my fiancé. I thought the meeting went well and she was aware of the closeness between my son and me.

The wedding happened as planned the next month. Four days after we said "I do", I received a letter from my lawyer that stated that my youngest child had told the child advocate that he desired to stay in Colorado and therefore my Ex and I would have a court trial next month. I was devastated at this news and broke down and cried hysterically. So many thoughts went through my head. How could this be happening? I had just married the man of my dreams. What should I do now? Should I stay and not sell my house in CO? Should I live here, away from my new husband that lives in the Midwest? That wasn't a way to start a marriage. Six years earlier my Ex left me and now was remarried. How was it that he could have an affair and change our family's lives and think this was an

OK thing to do? How was any of this fair? Oh, there it is, that word *fair.* I told my kids for years that life isn't fair. Once again I was experiencing another misfortune in my life. This seemed like a bad dream. No, a nightmare! Wake me up! Wake me up, please!

Well, there was a trial coming up, so I prepared by asking people that knew both of us to write letters stating why they thought I should remain the residential parent. I was excited that I had received several letters. I asked many to pray for the upcoming court case.

I flew back to Co for the court day. My very dear friend went with me for moral support. My ex chose to present me with some plea bargaining before going before the judge, stating if I 'give in' to letting our son remain living in CO, I don't have to pay my 'ex' back about $5,500 in overpaid child support from our oldest son turning 18 in the fall of his senior year in high school. I didn't accept his plea bargain! My child wasn't for sale! I did learn that my lawyer had been laid up with back pain days previously, but managed to attend the court hearing. Looking back, I wondered how many pain killers he was on during the trial. I sat next to him at the table and wondered why he didn't speak up more. I hadn't been in court before, so I didn't know what to do. I had the letters from my friends stacked nicely in front of me and ready to be presented to the judge. While sitting there a feeling came over me that I wasn't supposed to show the letters. So, they just sat there. I never shared the letters with the judge. I don't remember how long the court session was, or all that was said, but I do remember hearing the judge say our son was to stay and live in CO with his Dad. I was to be allowed to have a lot of time with him since I had been the residential parent. He was to spend the school year with his Dad and many of the holidays and summers with me. The judge said it was a guideline, but that we could work out more time as to what was best for our son. I walked out of the courtroom with my friend in an absolute daze of what had just happened. Did I hear him right? Did he really say my child wasn't coming with me? How can this be? The bottom of my world fell out. How was I supposed to move forward? I hated that my Ex won! It was downright evil! It's was so unfair! Yes, I'll say it again, *unfair*!

How was this justice after all that my Ex had already put me through?

I had to accept the reality of the situation. The only positive thing at the time was that it was summer and my son would be spending it with me. I couldn't be mad at him for feeling the way that he did. He was a scared 12-year-old boy that didn't want to leave all that he knew and was familiar to him. We had a wonderful summer together! But, it would come to an abrupt and sad end when I had to take him back to Colorado in the middle of August. Leaving him was one of the hardest things I've ever done as a mother.

Here I was the new girl in town, marrying the tall handsome bachelor and leaving her child behind. That's what it may have looked like to those who didn't know my story. I'm certain people thought there had to be a very good reason why the Dad had the child the majority of the time. I wonder what she did that caused the judge to not choose her to raise her son. How could she move away from her child for a man? Who leaves their child? Now, I don't know that people actually thought these thoughts, but in my head I believed they did. I felt like such a loser as a mother.

I was depressed and miserable. I felt such an injustice by not having my son with me. I missed my child and still couldn't believe that we weren't together! I was angry! I wept every day for several weeks that we weren't together. I tried to hide my sadness from my husband, because I didn't want him to feel guilty or responsible. His love for me gave me a reason to feel better when I wasn't miserable. If I had thought that there was any chance that my child wouldn't have moved with me, I think I would have waited to remarry. But, I just couldn't imagine my son not being with me. It was confusing because I believe God brought my husband and me together, but yet this union separated my son and me. How could this be a part of God's plan too? It was a lot to wrap my head around. My heart was in a joyous and painful conflict.

Nearly each month I visited my son. I wanted to make it easier on him too, since he was used to us living together his entire life thus far. If he had a soccer game, I'd try to make sure to schedule my visit so I could watch him play. When I'd fly to Colorado, he'd stay with me at a friend's house for the weekend. We'd play board games and ping pong, watch movies and go out to eat at our favorite places and spend time with his siblings if they were around. We spent quality time together. I soaked up every moment that I could with him, knowing it had to last me a few weeks. These visits and cell phone calls helped make the times I was separated from him more bearable.

We made it through the next six years and after high school graduation he came to live with me and my husband. We talked about his choice to stay in CO all those years ago and he told me "It was very hard not having you and Dad living in the same state. When you visited me, and when I'd stay the summer with you, we made some good memories. I was able to live in two households that loved me. Some people don't even get one. I think it helped that I was younger and didn't remember you and Dad being together. I think it made it easier for me because I see that you're both happy."

My son telling me this opened my eyes. I was so afraid he'd be scarred for life. But, he seemed to handle it better than I did. I was hard on myself when I listened to the lies that Satan would whisper to me, "Some kind of mother you are! Who deserts their son for a man? You're just a part-time Mom!" These were some of the lies I heard in my mind and it made me depressed quite often. Over these past several years, I wasn't angry at God. I knew that it happened because of sinful and prideful choices of his Dad and me. There are consequences to our decisions when they don't align with what God says in the Bible about how to live our lives. I asked God to show me what lesson I needed to learn as I walked that journey. He helped me to see that He provided for me by giving me a loving and understanding husband who encouraged me and financially paid for me to visit with my son each month. God helped my son to appreciate both households. God helped me to be able to work things out with his Dad, so I could visit each month during the school year. And, mostly, He helped me to see that in spite of the circumstances of the court decision, I am a loving mother and my son knows that he means the world to me.

I will never understand why this happened the way that it did, but I do know that I grew closer to God through the experience. It doesn't mean that I liked the journey, but I continued to believe that God knows what's best. *"For I know the plans I have for you, declares the Lord, plans for welfare and not for evil, to give you a future and a hope. Then you will call upon me and come and pray to me, and I will hear you. You will seek me and find me when you seek me with all your heart."* Jeremiah 29:11-13

He has a purpose and a plan for me and my son. He has one for you too!

Irony

I'm in one of the many rooms waiting to meet my new doctor. He comes in and has a nice demeanor about him. We talk about my medical file for a few minutes, than he says, *"I read in your files about your car accident in 2004 where you had a serious brain injury called an Axonal Shearing and a brain hemorrhage. I was wondering before I walked into the room and met you if you were alone, or if you were able to talk or walk, or if you were in some type of vegetative state. It was such a traumatic brain injury!"*

I was surprised and a bit taken back by what I just heard! I said, "Not one doctor has EVER said ANYTHING like this before to me! It's God! I've lived in different places, so many people were praying for my husband and me. I call it a *miracle!*"

It was the Monday evening before Thanksgiving when I climbed into my husband's truck. We were one day short of being married six months. Being newlyweds, I moved closer to him on the bench seat and buckled up. We took off down our driveway heading to meet some friend's, but we never made it to our destination.

Here's the email that was sent out by our minister at the time, *"Last evening Larry and Anna were in an auto accident where Route 3 and 143 intersect to get onto the Berm Highway around 6:30 p.m. A lady pulled in front of Larry's truck making an illegal left turn. Larry hit her and his pickup was stopped by a steel pole and both of them have suffered injury. Larry's hip and knee*

206

injuries will require a special kind of surgery that only one doctor at Barnes Jewish Hospital is able to perform. He has several others in front of him, so it may be a couple of days before he is operated on. I am not sure what the injuries are to his hip and left knee. Anna, as of this morning was still in the emergency room. She seems to have no overt injuries to her body. However, she is not responding and remains in what seems like a light coma. I have no medical information that this is a coma. Robin is staying with her, and she say's all Anna's done is sleep and open her eyes now and then. This is all the information that we have. Please remember them in your prayers."

It was Tuesday night when I actually woke up in the hospital unsure of where I was and what had happened to me. I remember my friend, Rhonda asking me if I wanted her to bring my boys to the hospital or to her house after she picked them up at the airport. It was that question that I believe "woke me up". I believe I was in a state of limbo, of unsureness of whether I wanted to live or die.

You see, it was just a few months ago that I left my youngest son in Colorado as I headed back to my new home in the Midwest. It was a time when I was depressed as a mother, because the court had awarded my son's dad with residential custody. It is my belief that my friend asking me that simple question helped me to realize that I would choose to live because of my children.

I still don't remember 24 hours of my life that began at that intersection where an 83-year-old lady turned left in a NO LEFT TURN intersection. We were going 45 mph and had the green light. Larry tried not to not hit her and just hit the side front of her car, which caused her car to spin around and out of our direction. We ricocheted off of her and hit a huge steel traffic light pole. Luckily, we were in a 1-ton pickup truck. Our truck was totaled and her little sedan was totaled. She walked away and didn't need to go to the hospital.

Larry and I weren't so lucky. I had a head injury and wasn't talking for about 24 hours. The doctor said that I "wasn't responding", so they ran tests and found that I had a very serious brain injury. I was conscious, but not self-aware. At times I would get up out of the bed, so I was put in a rubber room to not cause harm to myself. I have no recollection of this or of my husband being wheeled down to my room to see if I would recognize him. He was on so much morphine because of his intensive injuries that to be moved to see me caused him a lot of pain. My doctors thought maybe if I saw him I would recognize him and talk. He told me he was sad that I didn't know who he was. He was afraid of what was going to happen to me and to us. Visitors came and went and I remember a few, but most of my hospital stay is still a blur to me. Many people were praying for us. Amazingly, four days after the accident I was released to go home after my MRI didn't show anything. What a blessing! It really was a miracle that I could go home so quickly, which just so happened to be the day after Thanksgiving! My family had driven to see us once they learned of the accident and I was able to spend some time with them when I arrived home.

Larry remained in the hospital because of his serious injuries. His right hip was shattered and his leg was dangling by ligaments and tendons. His knee was broken and the knee cap was forced up about 3". He had surgery and a plate with eleven pins was put in his hip and two pins were put in his knee to hold his leg together. He was told that he may not walk again because of the intensity of the injury to his hip. He was crushed from hearing this news, but determined to prove them wrong.

Since this was our first Christmas together as a married couple I wanted to get the house decorated before he came home from the hospital. Some guys from church came over and helped me set up our Christmas tree because I wasn't supposed to lift much weight to cause strain on my body. After he had healed pretty well from surgery, he was moved to a rehabilitation hospital. It was there that he developed a blood clot and was moved to another hospital. Overall, he made decent progress considering the severity of his injuries and finally came home after 15 days. He was surprised to see the house decorated for Christmas and said, "It was the most beautiful Christmas tree he'd ever seen!" I'm not sure that was totally true, but I believe it was true at that moment in time. It was so nice to have him home.

Although, having him home brought about its own challenges. He couldn't bend his knee because of his injuries to his right leg. I figured out that in order for him to sit down and ride comfortably, I needed to remove the second seat in the van, so he could sit in the rear seat to keep his leg fully extended. I failed to mention that he's 6 feet 4 inches tall. His height just added to the challenge of not only fitting into vans, but bathtubs too. We made adjustments as needed. He got around pretty well with his walker at home. When we went out, he used a wheelchair because it was best for him since he tired easily. In the midst of everything, I decided to quit my job and stay at home to care for him. He could hardly do much of anything for himself at home and he also had many medical appointments that he needed me to take him to. He couldn't put weight on his right leg for a couple of months. He was slowly making progress, which made us both happy.

Shortly after the accident, I began experiencing headaches on the left side of my head throughout the day. My eyesight had also been affected from my head injury as well. Five years earlier I had Lasik eye surgery to correct the distance in both of my eyes. I discovered that I was now seeing up close with my left eye, but not long distance. Two eye specialists both told me that it could be corrected with Lasik, but said that many people request mono-vision. So, I decided to leave my eyes this way. It took a little getting used to, but I'm glad that I now have mono-vision. I went to the chiropractor up to three times a week to have adjustments to help my recurring headaches. The headaches lightened up five months after the accident. I still continue to visit my chiropractor regularly.

There's more to this story that made it much more difficult to handle. The elderly lady who caused the accident by turning in front of us belonged to the same church as us. It's highly unlikely that in a congregation of 250 members that we would both happen to be in the same intersection at the same time, especially when that intersection wasn't a road that we traveled often. It really was unbelievable! When we discovered who the driver of the other vehicle was, Larry was pleased that he had hit her car in such a way to move her away from getting hurt. He said if he would have hit her straight on, it would've been difficult for him to live with because she could've been killed.

It was a challenge for me to see this woman drive up to church in her new car when Larry was recovering in the hospital. I know she didn't intentionally cause the accident, and she felt badly about it, but, right then it didn't help me. She sent us many cards and offered peace offerings with plates of cookies. I wished it had been someone else that caused the accident, because it made it difficult since we went to church with her. Larry and I were concerned because she didn't have enough auto insurance coverage to pay our medical bills. His one surgery alone was $48K. We cringed when the bills arrived in our mailbox. There were so many that I made a carrying file box just for the accident. Larry had to have a custom made leg brace to sleep in that was expensive, considering his height. There were still treatments and physical therapy that he needed too! What were we going to do?

It was hard to understand God's plan and purpose with the accident. Now, I don't believe He caused it. No, she chose to drive and got confused about the traffic signs. She probably shouldn't have been driving, especially when it was dark outside. Why couldn't she have had better insurance coverage? We weren't going to sue her, but we sure wanted our bills to be paid. And, with Larry's injuries it was certain that he would need a knee and hip replacement later in life. Why shouldn't her insurance cover those medical expenses in the future? It was obvious that Larry and I had to work on forgiveness.

We decided it was best to hire a lawyer. We had no intentions of suing her, but we needed help with both of our insurance companies when it came to paying our medical bills. We were paying for five hospital stays between us. Thankfully, Larry had accumulated enough vacation time to still get paid his monthly income for over three months. Larry learned how to sell on eBay and did well selling items to help earn a little money and give him something to do. Sitting still was not something that he did much. I made frequent trips to the post office to mail his packages. In the meantime, we were served collection notices and our credit rating dropped, because we couldn't pay all of the medical bills on time. We were waiting for the insurance companies to pay. This wasn't our fault! Why was this happening? It just wasn't right! It took nearly two years before the lawyers settled with the doctors and

210

hospitals for all of our hospital stays. Our medical bills were finally paid, which we were very happy about, but our lives were forever changed. There was nothing left over to compensate for our injuries, especially Larry's. Any future surgeries would be out of our pockets.

I don't blame God, although sometimes I wonder about his plan and purpose. God doesn't ask me to understand, only to trust and have faith that He's going to take care of us. *"I do know that all things work together for good for those who love God and are called according to his purpose."* Romans 8:28.

We could've been less fortunate. I'm thankful for the big truck we were in and for wearing our seatbelts. I'm thankful for Larry's banked vacation time. Those were all wonderful provisions! We experienced early on in our marriage what the marriage vow 'in good times and in bad times' entailed. We agreed that it was a true test of our love and commitment to one another. We learned not to take anything for granted because we're not promised tomorrow.

Our attitudes improved the more mobile Larry became. It became easier to smile and greet the sweet elderly lady when we were at church. Several years after the accident, I had the opportunity to sing at her funeral, along with some others from church. As I sat at her funeral service, I was reminded of our accident. I grinned because it was ironic that I was singing for her. I never would've imagined it happening. It didn't happen because I'm an amazing person. It happened because I serve an awesome God! He helped me to learn about love and mercy because He showed it to me first by giving up His Son on the cross (read John 3:16).

There wasn't a penny left after paying all of our medical bills. We felt like our hands were tied in this situation. How we chose to react could affect many people at church. Larry and I talked and prayed, and talked and prayed some more. We were at the Lord's mercy in how to handle it. We learned it's best to remain quiet and let the good Lord work. *"The Lord will fight for you while you keep silent."* Exodus 14:14 NASB

Chapter 24

Transformation

When bad things happen in our lives, it can traumatize us. Satan wants us to think we can't get through it. He wants us to feel defeated, discouraged, lonely, miserable and mostly, hopeless. But, God has other plans! Surprise! The line's not been drawn, the game's not over and the lights aren't out. God loves to change Satan's agenda! Although we may not see the big picture, He does. We only see a puzzle piece, but He sees how all of the pieces fit together. He's been changing Satan's evil plans since the beginning of time in the Garden of Eden.

It's good to remember that Satan always loses and God is always the Victor! This doesn't mean we won't go through many emotions when life throws us a curve-ball. Some things that happen in our lives are difficult to understand. Every person is, has, or will go through some difficult times in life. Time doesn't stand still because your husband cheats on you, or your child goes off to war, or you're told that you have cancer. Life goes on. Time continues to move forward.

In these wound stories we've seen many ladies' hurts, but we've also seen their growth because of their relationship with Christ. I'd like to compare the journey that we've been on to that of a caterpillar. We casually walk through life and then one day, 'BAM', our life as we know it changes. Maybe it's something we did or that someone did to us or we get a diagnosis that's really no one's fault. Whatever it is, we know from this day forward our life has changed and we'll never be the same.

When the caterpillar is in the chrysalis stage it's being transformed from a caterpillar into a butterfly. When it's time, it struggles to break free from the cocoon. It pushes and a tiny rip is made. It continues to make the opening larger, and as it does, it's pushing the fluid out of its body and into its wings, so it can fly. It can take 8-13 days to free itself during this final stage. What if the butterfly decided it didn't want to do the work that was needed and it remained inside because it was afraid to emerge? What if someone watched it struggle to get out of the cocoon, decided to cut it open and enable the butterfly to come out without doing the work? In reality, the butterfly would have a swollen body and small, shriveled wings that would never spread open. It would spend the rest of its life crawling around on the ground. It would never fly.

There are some of you who are hurting right now and want to give up. Hang in there. God loves you and will walk you through it if you ask Him to help guide you. Instead of doing what you think is best, ask God to show you His purpose in the trial and to give you wisdom to handle it. The greatest tragedy in this life is when we choose to be the victim and never learn or rise above our problems. We never allow ourselves to live and learn and make the most of our lives. We become stuck where we are, not living the life that God designed for each one of us. It's similar to the butterfly who had help to get out of the cocoon instead of enduring the struggle, and now will spend its life on the ground, instead of spreading its wings and flying as it was created to do.

Choose to live your life to its fullest. Move through the tough times and learn from the experience. One of my favorite Bible verses that I share often and the main reason for me writing this book is found in 2 Corinthians 1:4-6 (NLT) *"He comforts us in all our troubles so that we can comfort others. When they are troubled, we will be able to give them the same comfort God has given us. [5] For the more we suffer for Christ, the more God will shower us with his comfort through Christ. [6] Even when we are weighed down with troubles, it is for your comfort and salvation! For when we ourselves are comforted, we will certainly comfort you. Then you can patiently endure the same things we suffer".* All the ladies life journey's told in this book are to help bring healing, understanding and mainly hope to hurting hearts.

Life hits us with different things. God doesn't cause it, but He can use it for our good. The devil brings misery, not God. I know all that I've been through has had a purpose. I've learned so much about myself and my faith in God. I don't have to understand, I only need to have faith, believe and follow Him. It has been in my struggles that I've learned that Jesus has the power to heal and offer hope beyond what I can comprehend. It doesn't mean everything's worked out as I wanted. Just like the caterpillar we will struggle to break free, believing there's something better to come. And, when we do, we can be transformed. Not into beautiful butterflies as the caterpillar, but, changed by knowing and being loved by God and His Son and seeing the change in ourselves. Titus 3:4-5 (NLT) *" But, when God our Savior revealed his kindness and love, [5] he saved us, not because of the righteous things we had done, but because of his mercy. He washed away our sins, giving us a new birth and new life through the Holy Spirit"*.

Are you ready for a transformation?

If any readers would like to connect with an author of a specific life story you may contact: AnnaKaySchmidt@gmail.com.

Please specify which chapter you're referring to and she may be able to make the connection with the author of that particular story and have her return your email.

Transformed   (Aimee's Song)

By Anna Kay Schmidt
In honor of my daughter, Aimee I. Herren,
who at age 16, had the courage to change.
Written March 17, 2002

	E F E D C D E
1st verse -	Life used to be so simple
	D D E F E D E D C
	you used to run and laugh and play
	D D E F E D C D E
	your smiles and laughter were contagious
	D E F E D C C
	you brought joy to every day.

	C F E D C D E
2nd	But now, your eyes are empty
	D D E F E D C C
	I look at you and no one's there
	D E F E D C D E
	As a mother I feel helpless.
	D D E F E D C C
	How do I let you know I care?

	A B C B A G G
Chorus 1:	When did life become so hard?
	F G A G F E F E-D
	That a hug just wouldn't do~
	D F E D C D
	to chase away your tears
	D D E FE D C C
	and bring a smile back to you?

3rd verse -   Life brought us many changes
              You chose new friends along the way~
              What they offered would not help you
              The stuff they gave you changed your ways.

4th   You lied to me, but I trusted
              Because my heart couldn't believe~
              That my sweet little Aimee
              found it so easy to deceive.

Chorus 2:   When did life become so hard,
              that your life is filled with grief?
              You've chosen alcohol and drugs
              to escape and find relief.

5th   As a mother I feel helpless
              to chase your blues away.
              Lord, show me how to reach her,
              show me this I pray.

6th   Then one day it happened
              A 12 step program changed your ways
              You found new friends to love and help you
              Make living with reality OK

Chorus 3:   When did life become so hard
              that the choices were so few?
              Although now you have some answers
              cause you 'let go and let God' see you thru.

8th verse   The road to recovery isn't easy
              Many tears were shed along the way~
              But when you work the program
              You know you can make it one more day.

9th verse   Your progress is amazing
Now you help others see~
That drugs aren't the answer -
No, the answers SO_BRIE_I_TY !
                   (sobriety)

Chorus 4:   Now that life is not so hard
You know you'll make it through
Cause' its really not so hopeless
when you have loving friends there for you.

End (slower)- Cause' you won't make it without your friends * and God * who'll see---you through.

CPSIA information can be obtained
at www.ICGtesting.com
Printed in the USA
FFHW011355020319
50711662-56139FF